THE PRINCETON REVIEW

Work Smart

To Abdul,

Good Luck as you conquer the ~~corpoak~~ corporate world. Thank-you for being such a good friend & part of my wedding.

6/20/99

P.S. I do not know where you get the energy!

THE PRINCETON REVIEW

Work Smart

250 Smart Moves Your Boss Already Knows

BY MARCI I. TAUB, M.A. AND
L. MICHELLE TULLIER, PH.D.

Random House, Inc.
New York 1998
www.randomhouse.com

Princeton Review Publishing, L.L.C.
2315 Broadway
New York, NY 10024
e-mail: info@review.com

ISBN 0-679-78388-1

Designer: Illeny Maaza
Production Editor: Kristen Azzara
Production Coordinator: Iam Williams

Manufactured in the United States of America

9   8   7   6   5   4   3   2   1

First Edition

Acknowledgments

Throughout my life, I've been fortunate to encounter many people who've taught me something valuable about managing my career. Some have said that they work to live, not live to work. Some have said that the most important thing is to find a way to do what you love—no matter what. And some have said that it isn't what you do to earn a living that matters; it's the values—like humility, integrity, responsibility, and respect for others—that you bring to your job and your life that are the most important things. By sending such diverse messages, these people have challenged me to consider what it really means to "work smart": achieving a balance between paid work and the rest of my life; using my natural gifts to the fullest; taking a value-driven approach to work; or some combination of these and other things. I've come to realize that it's not an either/or choice, and have incorporated aspects of all of these approaches into my personal philosophy. I'm grateful to everyone who has helped me to keep learning how to work smart. My most important guides have included my family—my husband, Adam Taub, my mother, Arlene Karetnick, my father, Harold Karetnick, my sister, Ellyn Karetnick, and my in-laws, Mel and Cheryl Taub; my friends—especially Cindy Crisp, Lisa Geller, Andrea Meyer, Tanja Sendak, Justin Sendak, Abbie Roth, Elissa Tomasetti, Dan Wiley, Michelle Weichert, and Steve Weichert; my mentors along the way—especially Edie Swan, Carolyn Stolper Friedman, Gloria Pierce, Irene Rosenzweig, and Karen Fine; and my colleague and friend Michelle Tullier.

—Marci Taub

Our thanks to Amy Bryant for her thoughtful editing and responsiveness. We are grateful to Evan Schnittman for making this project a reality. We appreciate Kathy Schneider's and Jeanne Krier's ongoing enthusiasm about *Work Smart*. A special thank you to Amy Zavatto for her support and early interest in this book. And many thanks to Dori Zuravicky for her expert research assistance.

—Marci Taub and Michelle Tullier

CONTENTS

PREFACE: WHAT MAKES THIS BOOK SPECIAL?

Work Smart was written to help you through the frustrating, confusing, or downright disastrous times that arise as you attempt to manage your job or career successfully. Whether you're a recent graduate just starting out in the working world, or you're in your twenties or thirties with some experience behind you, *Work Smart* is for you.

We simply want to teach you how to work smart. You might be struggling with office politics or a difficult boss, facing ethical dilemmas, wondering how to get a promotion, or deciding if you should change your career field. To help you deal with these and many other issues, we've included over 250 tips called *Smart Moves*, that will help you do the job right and get ahead in your career.

Many career management books offer advice only for people who are working in the corporate world. They usually refer to your employer as "your company" and discuss things like "corporate culture." We know that there's a lot more to the work world than corporations, so this book is designed to help you work smart in any type of environment. Whether you work for a not-for-profit organization, government agency, or a corporation, you will be able to adapt the advice on these pages to your situation. This book will also help those of you working outside of the traditional 9 to 5 world, as temps, consultants, contract workers, and freelancers.

Also, many career management books give very generalized advice and focus too heavily on trends in management theory. This book, however, provides you with concrete strategies that you can use right away—not just abstract theories. Having worked as career counselors, professors, and consultants with thousands of recent graduates and young professionals, we based the information you'll find in this book on what has worked for real people.

And finally, we didn't just want to give you cookie-cutter advice about how to handle the issues that come up on the job or in your career path. The guidelines in *Work Smart* are flexible enough that you can personalize them for your specific situation. So you can use this book as a primer when you're starting a new job, as a resource when you're stuck on how to resolve a workplace issue, and as a companion when you're considering leaving a job or changing your career field.

The advice is grouped into three broad categories: How to Look, Think, and Act on the Job; How to Get Ahead; and How to Change Careers. The categories were developed based on our clients' most commonly asked questions. The three parts of this book don't necessarily represent a linear progression of lessons you will learn in your career. So, we encourage you to skip around and turn to the chapters that are relevant from day-to-day on your job or in your overall career planning. Within each part you'll find topics clustered thematically, so that you can easily find and get advice about specific issues.

You'll also find quizzes to test your "Work Smart IQ," exercises to put the Smart Moves into action, and some sidebars for comic relief and extra tips. And, the appendix refers you to lots of helpful books and websites for additional information to help you manage your career more successfully.

INTRODUCTION: WHY IS IT SO HARD TO WORK SMART?

CHALLENGE: WORKING SMARTER, NOT HARDER

Kaitlin had just landed her first job out of college. Initially, she felt incredibly relieved, figuring that the hard part was over. But as she approached her first day of work, a sense of anxiety replaced her feeling of relief. Kaitlin's manager had told her that she got the job mainly because of her stellar performance as a summer intern. But she didn't know how to transform herself from "that intern from ABC University" into a professional. Kaitlin was secretly concerned that her manager would expect her to be able to jump in and make major contributions right away. She let this assumption undermine her self-confidence. Kaitlin worried that she would get fired by the end of the month.

Matt had worked in his current position for a little over eighteen months. He was a fast learner and easily mastered the technical aspects of his job. At his one-year performance review, his manager assured him that he was doing really well. For about the last six months, Matt noticed a change in his relationship with his manager. His manager was not giving him the same kind of glowing feedback, or opportunities to take on more responsibility. On the one hand, Matt reasoned that his manager was traveling more than usual and therefore not fully aware of his achievements. On the other hand, even when his manager wasn't in the office, he often had to clean up Matt's messes. Matt was unhappy about his fall from grace, but he couldn't get a handle on how to remedy the situation.

Tyra was employed by the same organization for five years. More and more, she woke up in the morning dreading her job, which she felt was a dead-end street. When she had started her job after college, she looked forward to going to work, and was really excited about her field. During the last two years, her senior managers had restructured her division three times. In the midst of all of this change, she lost her passion. Tyra wasn't even sure whether she was disillusioned about her organization, her field, or both. And she didn't know what to do to get out of her rut.

STARTING WITH YOU

Working smart can be confusing, especially for a recent graduate or young professional. Issues that Kaitlin, Matt, and Tyra faced, such as making the transition from being an intern to being an employee, navigating office politics, and handling workplace changes are only a few of the difficult challenges you might face on the job.

Smart Move #1: Expect to Deal With Ambiguous Situations Every Day

As you progress in your career, you'll discover that you will need to handle ambiguous situations constantly. For instance, how can you continuously understand the nature and scope of your responsibilities, interact effectively with others, get things done, decide how much risk to take, or know when and how to leave your job? It's a constant challenge to figure out what to do and how to do it in a way that advances your career. As frustrating as this reality may seem, it's just part of the nature of being a successful professional in a rapidly changing work world.

Smart Move #2: Put What Motivates You in Your Job

What motivates you directly affects your ability to work smart. Both your values and circumstances determine what motivates you on the job. On the values side, for example, you may define success as holding a job that will allow you to pursue your hobbies after hours and on the weekends. Or, you may get really excited when you're doing paid work for a social cause that you care about. Maybe you may need to achieve progressively higher levels of responsibility, power, and compensation to feel successful. Perhaps intellectual stimulation and creative opportunities are the most important aspects of a job for you.

For better or worse, your circumstances also motivate you. Financial hardships, such as paying back undergraduate student loans, financing graduate school, and supporting yourself and/or your family, can compel you to succeed on your job. Pressure from your family to succeed in a certain field or with a particular organization can also push you to do well. (Remember, though, that succumbing to this pressure may make your family happy, but it may make *you* miserable.) Whatever motivates you—and this is likely to change over time—you need to understand and prioritize both your values and needs carefully. Often, this may mean that you must temporarily choose between two important values and needs, or among several of your top values and needs. (See chapter 7 for more on defining your priorities.)

Smart Move #3: Maximize Your Learning Style

Knowing your learning style can also help you to succeed. You may learn most effectively through first reading about, talking about, or trying out a skill. There's no wrong way to learn. The key is to understand your preferred style of learning and then to seek learning opportunities that complement your style.

Sometimes you'll have a helpful (or not so helpful) manager with a style of learning that's different from yours. For example, your manager may expect you to learn how to use a new software program by reading the documentation. If your preferred learning style is to have someone explain something to you, then you may want to take a crash course for the program in a classroom, by videotape, or in a virtual classroom on the Internet. If you're more comfortable "learning by doing," you could get a tutorial for the software. A tutorial will take you through the basics right on your computer. If you have the time, you could even play around with the program until you get the hang of it.

Once you've used your preferred learning style, then you can draw upon other methods to enhance your learning. So if you're primarily a hands-on learner, you can first try something out, and then either talk about it with someone who has more advanced knowledge, or read more about it. If you like to read in-depth about a new skill, you may want to try it out first or listen to an expert speak about it.

At some point, all three methods—reading, talking, and trying—will play a role in your learning process. It's really a matter of leading with your strength. Make it easy on yourself and go with what works best for you. You'll learn faster and have more fun doing it.

Smart Move #4: Blend Your Decision-Making Approach With Those of Others

Every day you make so many decisions in both your professional and personal life that you may not even realize how you go about the decision making. Some tend to make snap decisions, either based on a black and white view of the world, or on pure gut instinct. Others typically take as much time as possible to make decisions, thoroughly considering every possible angle and outcome. Many of us do not approach decision making strictly one way or the other. But it's very important to recognize your favorite approach and to be aware of how it matches or clashes with others, especially your manager's.

So, yes, it's hard to work smart because of the many forces that you need to contend with on an ongoing basis. The good news is that by using the Smart Moves we present in *Work Smart*, you can better manipulate these forces to work your way.

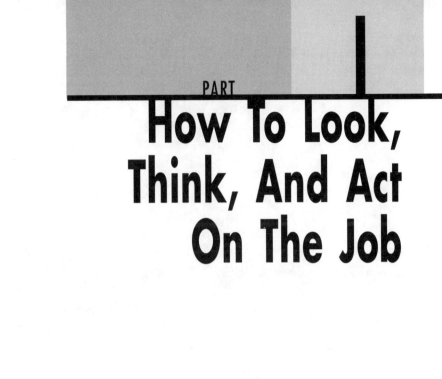

PART

How To Look, Think, And Act On The Job

CHAPTER 1

Developing A Professional Identity

WORK SMART IQ QUIZ #1

Review each item below and decide if it's a work smart myth or a work smart reality. In the space before each statement, put an "M" if you think it's a myth and an "R" if you think it's a reality. Then check your responses with the correct answers at the end of the quiz.

_____ **1.** There's no real way to be sure how you come across to others, so you may as well just not think about it and focus on your work.

_____ **2.** The best way to succeed is to concentrate most heavily on the details of your job responsibilities.

_____ **3.** Keeping on top of trends in your industry, and the world in general, can help you get ahead.

_____ **4.** Your level of personal success directly corresponds to how high you rise in your career field.

_____ **5.** You should treat everyone you come in contact with—both inside and outside of your organization and at all levels—as a client.

_____ **6.** Admit mistakes and take responsibility for them right away.

_____ **7.** Leaving a brief phone message is more important than leaving a specific one.

_____ **8.** E-mail is a confidential means of communicating at work.

_____ **9.** Where and how you sit and your body language can make or break your participation in a meeting.

_____ **10.** The only way to stop or recover from burnout is by going into therapy.

IMAGE

CHALLENGE: MANAGING OTHERS' PERCEPTIONS OF YOU

Devin's friends gave him the nickname "The Joker" when he was fifteen. By the time he graduated from college, he had a long history of staging practical jokes and telling wild stories that made everyone laugh. During Devin's job search, he charmed and amused his interviewers. He knew just how to find the humor in a situation without being inappropriate. This attribute helped him to land his dream job.

Once on the job, Devin's quick wit initially helped him to bond with his coworkers and manager. However, he became overly dependent on his humor to mask his occasional discomfort. Devin provoked others by responding in a sarcastic tone of voice and rarely giving straight answers to difficult questions. Others perceived him as a slacker—someone who didn't pay attention to serious matters.

Lydia was always labeled an overachiever. Growing up, adults often commented that she was both precocious and driven. She always did extra credit projects and took the maximum number of advanced classes. She spent every summer in school, learning a new language or reading books for the following year's curriculum. Lydia graduated at the top of her class and entered college with so many credits that she graduated in three years.

Her image as a fast tracker followed her into her first job after college. She took advantage of every opportunity to learn—taking home extra reading every night, going in early to initiate new projects, and signing up for related continuing education classes. Her manager and peers were impressed by her commitment. But Lydia neglected the other elements that it takes to develop a professional identity. For example, she was so focused on the tasks required by her job that she wasn't very friendly with her colleagues. She missed the crucial window of opportunity as the new kid to build strong professional relationships. When she finally realized this, it was much harder for her to develop connections. Others viewed her as hyper-competitive, rather than cooperative and a fast tracker. In addition, Lydia neglected every other aspect of her life. For example, she rarely gave herself a break, even on the weekends. By the end of her first year of work, she found that she couldn't keep up her supersonic work pace, and began to develop an accurate reputation as a burnout.

MAKING YOURSELF OVER INSIDE-OUT

Humorist, Slacker, Fast-Tracker, Burnout—these may seem like high school labels, but in all spheres of your life you have an image that is as apparent to others as a yearbook tagline. As Devin and Lydia found out, your image is especially powerful in the workplace because it can make or break your career.

Smart Move #5: Define Your Perceived and Real Images

What image do you think you currently project at work? Why? The best way to figure out how you're coming across to others is to ask. But it may not be appropriate or feel comfortable for you to ask people you don't know well how you are perceived. So ask someone you work closely with (who you're also friendly with) to let you know how they think others see you. Depending on how your organization conducts performance reviews, you may get a broader range of feedback from people in different areas and at different levels of your organization, and you may get some surprising responses.

You may discover that others don't perceive you in the same way that you perceive yourself. For example, Devin saw himself as a humorist, while others perceived him as a joker and a fool. Lydia saw herself as a fast tracker, while others perceived her as a burnout. You may find out that your professional image varies depending upon how well someone knows you, their position in the organization, or their level. In any case, it's important for your success that you find out why your imagined and real images are different at work.

Smart Move #6: Determine Why You May Have a Perception Gap

Sometimes perception gaps have to do with seemingly minor things that you do without a second thought. For example, you may be the hardest working person on your floor. But you spend too much time schmoozing with colleagues by the water cooler or while getting coffee. Everyone knows that you're friendly and fun to talk with, but they don't realize that you're productive. So be discreet and conservative about taking breaks during the day for coffee, smoking, or other extraneous things.

Maybe you work all day with your door closed and you consistently produce high quality work before your deadlines, but make little or no regular contact with your coworkers. They're hesitant to knock on your door and interrupt you. At your mid-year performance review, you're shocked to discover that others have reported that you're aloof and inaccessible. In this situation, it's important for you to find a better balance between your closed and open door time.

Another common problem concerns work hours. You need to be in tune with your organization's and boss's expectations of your work hours. Some places have fixed hours, though most professionals exceed them anyway. In some organizations, it's okay to walk out the door when the clock strikes the closing hour of the day. In most situations, though, you'll need to put in some extra time at the beginning and/or end of your typical workday.

This extra time isn't just about getting your work done. You may be a really efficient worker who finishes tasks in record time. Nevertheless, it's important that you show your face with the rest of the crew. Pace yourself to stretch out your work during the day.

Another approach is to find extra things to do early in the morning or late in the day that don't require much brain power. Use this time to catch up on professional reading, Internet scanning, filemaking, or other routine tasks that have to get done anyway.

How you hand in your work also determines your image. Going the extra step to hand in neat, presentable projects will boost your reputation as a thorough, professional worker. Many offices have incorporated software that makes this process easier than ever. Also, the quality of the paper, report cover, and even the binder clips can make a difference. But be careful to format your work without going over budget. Even in larger, wealthier industries, organizations are watching their bottom lines on increasingly micro levels. So check out what's acceptable before you get slammed for it.

Who you befriend on the job can also help or hinder your professional reputation. No matter how well you do your job, the people you become associated with reflect your judgment and character. Don't join the first clique you come across. It may not be the group you want to be associated with later on.

Keep your on-the-job relationships friendly, but professional. It's okay to socialize with people who you find fun or have things in common with outside of work. In fact, it may help you bond with your colleagues to hang out occasionally after work with groups of peers for dinner or drinks. Just remember that what you share during happy hour may come back to haunt you during work hours. So keep it simple—no telling tales about coworkers, complaining about your manager, or sharing inside information about high-profile projects.

Smart Move #7: Alter or Strengthen Your Real Image

Image Exercise

Directions: Write down the image you think that you are currently projecting on the job, and what specific behaviors determine this image. Then, decide what image you want to project, whether it's different or not, and what behaviors will help you to create and maintain this image. Even if your current and ideal images match, try to come up with some new ways to enhance this image. Then use the behaviors related to your ideal image as the basis for an action plan to reinforce or make over your workplace image.

Current Image:

Why is this your image? (Your current behavior—related to downtime, accessibility, work hours, quality of work, job friends, etc.):

1.

2.

3.

4.

5.

Ideal Image:

How can you go about attaining this image? (Your future behavior—related to down time, accessibility, work hours, quality of work, job friends, etc.):

1.

2.

3.

4.

5.

The Smart Moves throughout the rest of the topics in this chapter—perspective, clients, attitude, protocol, clothes, humor, and burnout—will further enable you to develop a professional image.

The Chameleon's Guide to Undesirable Image-Making

Become a master of disguise and keep them guessing about who you'll show up as one day to the next. That way you won't get stuck with any one image for very long. Here's a sample week of undesirable images to try on:
Monday: The Egotist
Tuesday: The Kiss Up Queen
Wednesday: The Over-The-Top-Friendly Guy
Thursday: The Doormat
Friday: The Over-Achiever

PERSPECTIVE

CHALLENGE: BALANCING THE FOREST AND THE TREES

Carly went through a rough period during her first year on the job. She was determined to master her specific responsibilities and she spent all of her energy making sure that she completed her work thoroughly and on time. When a hot issue came up at a department, division, or organizational staff meeting, or when a new industry merger took place, she often felt like the only one who didn't anticipate it happening. Her colleagues rarely seemed surprised at major happenings. Bewildered, Carly wasn't sure what to do to keep on top of things.

Phil changed his career field seven times in the five years since he'd graduated from college. He changed direction often because he wasn't sure what he really wanted to do with his life. Finally, he decided on a field that was best for him, and started a related part-time job. He also took a couple of related continuing education classes at a local university. Phil's three closest friends were very supportive of what he was doing, but he still felt embarrassed and like a failure. His friends were all advancing to the next level in their professions, while he was just beginning to pursue one seriously.

Barbara worked really hard for seven years, and her manager rewarded her with three promotions. During Barbara's recent performance review, her manager shared his intention to train her to take over his job in a year. While she was flattered, she also felt dismayed. Lately, she'd realized that she wasn't necessarily interested in moving up any further. She was tired of running from one meeting to another and working twelve- to fourteen-hour days. Her hectic schedule meant that she often had to skip going to the gym or cancel dinner plans with her boyfriend at the last minute. But she wasn't sure whether she should trade off the opportunity to move up for a more well-rounded lifestyle. She was uncomfortable with staying in her current position or a similar one at the same level. It went against everything she'd ever learned about becoming successful.

UNDERSTANDING HOW EVERYTHING IS CONNECTED

Which is more important—the forest or the trees? The correct answer is both. Many recent grads and young professionals like Carly, Phil, and Barbara focus on the trees, or the details required by their particular jobs at the moment. But to grow as a professional, you've got to keep the big-picture in mind at all times. Getting the hang of your job is an obvious move. What may not be as evident is that you need to understand how your job relates to everything around it in your professional and personal life.

Smart Move #8: Locate Your Job as a Bullseye

One key aspect of the forest perspective is to understand how your job fits into the rest of your organization and field. Think of your job as the center of a small circle that's surrounded by several concentric circles. The next larger circle is your department. How does your job fit into your department's mission? Both when you interview for a job and as you begin one, your manager will mention something about the role you'll play in your department. It's likely that she'll focus on your and your coworkers' job descriptions. So you may know up front about the basics of what you're supposed to do and what those around you are doing.

But you need to know more about how things fit together, and it's probably up to you to fill in the gaps. For example, what are your manager's short- and long-term goals for your department? How does your manager rank these goals in priority order? What pending factors may affect the nature or importance of these goals in the near future? How does your manager expect your individual performance goals to help achieve the department's goals? Which of your responsibilities overlap with your colleagues? In what ways should you work together on a regular or as-needed basis?

Your division is the second circle out. How does your department work as a unit within your division? The third circle is the organization. What is the role of your division within the organization as a whole? Fourth comes your field. How does the organization function in the scheme of your field? Your industry is the largest circle. What are the current trends in your industry that affect your organization? Use professional association events, journals, newsletters, and the like to keep up with current trends in your field and industry. Always make sure you know how what you're doing is part of the bigger picture and, conversely, how each of the happenings in the larger circles affects your job.

Smart Move #9: Measure Your Professional Success by Your Cumulative Achievements

That often asked question, "What do you want to be when you grow up?" is not only challenging, but sometimes disturbing. It implies that your ultimate success is determined by how soon you define and attain your career goals. The reality is that many people don't know what profession they really want to pursue right away. And, due to the ever changing work world, it's likely that you'll change your career field at least a few times during your lifetime. You may judge yourself harshly based on how little progress you believe you've made towards establishing the career of your dreams. If this sounds familiar, stop putting yourself down right now. Reevaluate your professional success based upon how far you've come, not how far you need to go. Even if you're not yet on, or are just beginning to follow, your dream career field path, you can take pride in the steps (however small) you've taken to get there. For example, finding an internship or part-time job, volunteering in your field of interest, taking a related course, learning the ropes in your first job, or gaining some relevant skills in a few different jobs, will all help you get what you want. This will help you feel accomplished and good about yourself. Making even the slightest effort will keep your progress in perspective and increase your motivation and energy for working smart.

Smart Move #10: Accept That It's Okay to Go Sideways

Another false perspective about success is that it correlates to how high you climb in your career field. Not everyone is capable or interested in devoting every waking moment to their jobs. If you do what you can (and want to) in your profession, that's enough. Many recent graduates and young professionals decide that it's more important to achieve a balance between their professional and personal lives than it is to rise to the top of their professions. And even some mid-career professionals are taking time out or simplifying their work lives to make room for family time, hobbies, and their health.

Smart Move #11: Redefine *Career* to Include All Aspects of Your Life

Many people have a *tree* perspective of what *career* means. They think that careers are only what they do to earn paychecks. This way of thinking can be limiting. A more realistic, constructive approach is to redefine *career* as everything someone does in his or her personal and professional worlds.

For example, from the time that you enter school to when you graduate from college, being a student is your career. And, if you hold a job, internship, or volunteer position during this time, these activities are part of your career too. At the same time, you're a daughter or son, possibly a sibling, friend, and maybe boyfriend, girlfriend, or spouse. You may also pursue hobbies on the side. All of these roles that you play in all aspects of your life can count as part of your career.

As a recent graduate and young professional, your family, friends, teachers, the media, and others, may refer only to your paid work as your career. But the reality is that everything you do in both your personal and professional lives collectively makes up your career.

When you redefine *career* in this way, you'll discover that there's less pressure on you to succeed only in your work life. When your professional life isn't moving in the right direction or moving ahead as fast as you'd like it to, you can reflect on your strides in other aspects of your life. They all contribute toward your growth and maturity as a person, and in turn will enhance your ability to be an effective professional.

Also, by redefining *career*, you can give yourself permission to explore a range of paid work options to support your genuine interest. For example, you may want to take a temporary job that you're overqualified for in order to have flexible or consistent work hours. This freedom will enable you to pay your bills while you pursue your dream of becoming an actor, a writer, the head of your own business, or while you go to graduate school. (See chapter 7 for advice on how to choose the right career field.)

CLIENTS

CHALLENGE: PRIORITIZING WHO'S IMPORTANT

Max arrived at work a half-hour early and breezed by his other early bird coworkers. He went straight to his desk, hoping to un-earth at least a corner of its surface by lunch time. Much to his dismay, he discovered five new voice mails, eight new e-mails, and three new faxes waiting for him from colleagues. He decided that he was too swamped with work to pay attention to these latest requests. Instead, he focused only on his backlog of projects, as well as new demands from outside clients. He plodded along like this until mid-afternoon. Then, at around 3:00 p.m., he paused momen-tarily to stretch his arms over his head. As he glanced up, Max noticed that his manager was walking briskly toward him with an angry look on her face. She told him that she'd received complaints about him all morning. She asked him why he hadn't replied to inside clients' urgent requests for information for the last seven hours. Max explained that he'd been too busy with external client work. His manager informed him that this approach was unaccept-able. She led Max into her office and closed the door. Then she reviewed all of his pending projects with him and ranked each task as to its relative importance. She instructed him to prioritize the most important requests and respond to them in a timely manner. And she told him to come to her immediately if he had trouble.

TREATING INSIDERS AND OUTSIDERS EQUALLY

One of the biggest mistakes you can make in your career is to treat your coworkers worse than you treat external or "official" internal clients. In fact, all of your colleagues within your organization count as clients. You should treat everyone you come in contact with (both inside and outside of your organization and at all levels) as a client.

Smart Move #12: Make Yourself Accessible

Everyone gets into a bad mood sometimes. Just make sure that you don't take your mood out on anyone else. It's not necessary to paste a fake smile on your face when you walk through the door. Demon-strate common courtesy by saying hello in a friendly tone of voice, smiling a little, and making eye contact. These little gestures will make others perceive you as a positive, approachable individual.

Smart Move #13: Return All Messages Promptly

Whether you receive phone calls, e-mail messages, or faxes, it's critical that you respond to them as quickly as possible. It may seem hard to juggle current projects, meetings, outside clients, and internal clients. But returning messages should be a priority, regardless of how busy you get.

Prioritize inside clients' messages over outside ones. Your inside clients often have vital information that will impact your performance. And this information often relates directly or indirectly to outside client issues. You need to establish and maintain solid relationships with your colleagues in order for both of you to succeed. It will also make your work environment more pleasant, since everyone appreciates it when you respect them enough to take their messages seriously.

Smart Move #14: Manage Your Time By Tuning In to Clients' Needs

The way to prevent phone, e-mail, and fax messages from taking up all of your time is to make your responses as considerate and productive as possible. If you focus on finding out what the other person really needs or is concerned about, you'll maximize your efforts. Keep in mind, especially with phone calls, that people have different communication styles. For example, you may be a cut-to-the-chase kind of phone caller, while the other person likes to make small talk at the beginning and end of the conversation. Try to accommodate the requester's style as much as possible (within reason). If someone is particularly chatty, you can still come across as responsive by taking a couple of minutes to indulge their banter. Then redirect the conversation back to the issue at hand.

Smart Move #15: Act and Follow Up Quickly and Consistently

Work with the client to determine what kind of solution will best meet their needs. Then let the client know what action you plan to take to resolve their problem (and by when). Finally, follow-up afterwards to determine that the outcome was successful. Instead of helping the client directly, sometimes you'll need to refer them to someone else. If this is the case, then arrange a conference call with the third party or walk the client to them if possible. This way you can facilitate a smooth transition without just handing the client off. You can also ensure that you're referring the client to the right source.

Smart Move #16: Share Relevant Information with Others

If you're working on a team project, it may be easy to get caught up in working on your piece. Keeping other team members informed about the latest developments that impact your work, is every team member's responsibility. Failing to communicate with others can backfire. For example, you and the others may work long and hard to complete a project only to discover that you're headed in the wrong direction. A significant piece of information that fell between the cracks would have enabled your group to stay on track, getting your work done well and on time.

Smart Move #17: Handle Conflicts Before They Handle You

Occasionally, conflicts will arise between you and a client. It may be tempting to ignore these tensions and hope that they resolve themselves. It's not worth the risk—they could grow rather than diminish. Since you never know when you may have to work with someone again, it's best not to let these kind of situations fester. Don't point fingers and throw blame around. Instead, address the problems directly, immediately, and constructively. Focus on the problem by sticking to the facts and focusing on how the other person's specific behaviors (words and actions) affected you without being accusatory. For example, say things like, "When you said 'Blah, blah, blah . . .' I felt really annoyed, because. . . ." Or "When you decided how to handle *abc* situation without my input, I was upset, because we were supposed to agree on what to do beforehand." Listen carefully to the other person's point of view without interrupting or judging what she's saying. Try to understand the situation from her perspective. And be prepared to respectfully disagree. You can then get past the situation and proceed.

Smart Move #18: Evaluate Your Level of Responsiveness

Client Exercise

Directions: To get a handle on how well you currently respond to clients' needs, keep a client response diary for a week. For every client's request that you receive, use the categories below to guide you in recording your specific behaviors and the outcomes. It may seem tedious at first, but it's an excellent way to gauge what you're really doing, and how you can improve and demonstrate your commitment to service excellence.

Sample Response Diary

Date:

Client Name:

Department:

Type of Request (E-mail, Fax, Phone, In-person):

Time of Request:

Specific Request:

Client's Communication Style (e.g., Verbal, Written, etc.):

Client's Desired Response Time Frame (e.g., two hours, three days, etc.):

Time Frame You and the Client Agreed Upon:

Specific Action(s) Taken to Address the Request (including referral to another resource if applicable) and Date/Time of Each Action:

Date/Time   Date/Time:

Step #1:   Step #2:

Follow-up Steps Taken with the Client and Date/Time of Each Step:

Date/Time: Date/Time:

Step #1:   Step #2:

Specific Outcome(s) of Actions (including client feedback):

Nature of Conflict(s) Along the Way (if applicable):

Content of Your Response to Conflict(s):

Style of Your Response to Conflict(s):

Outcome of Conflict(s):

Areas for Improvement (your turn-around time at any point in the process, follow up, handling conflict, etc.):

Five Sure-fire Ways To Alienate Clients

1) *Delete or toss any requests that sound boring or inconvenient at the time. Then pretend that you never received them, surmising that it was a high-tech snafu.*
2) *Wait at least 72 hours—or until your manager comes after you—(whichever comes first) to respond to phone calls, faxes, and e-mails.*
3) *Always pass client inquiries on to someone else by opening your rolodex and picking someone out randomly.*
4) *When clients seem frantic or pushy, assume that it's their problem and act rudely to shut them up.*
5) *When you have a conflict with a client, instigate a shouting match. Or don't deal with the situation at all and make excuses for avoiding them in the future as much as possible.*

ATTITUDE

CHALLENGE: APPROACHING YOUR JOB

Monika was a self-proclaimed realist. She prided herself on quickly recognizing what was getting in the way of making a situation successful. She was the one on every team project to identify the obstacles. However, when her manager gave her an individual assignment, the first words out of Monika's mouth were, "Yes, but...." Monika thought that she had a great attitude and that she was perceived as a valuable asset to her organization. Others saw Monika as smart and capable of making a difference. But they considered her to be essentially a pessimist because Monika approached obstacles as problems, rather than as challenges. She talked so much about the problems (rather than about the possible solutions) that she got bogged down by them. Monika's colleagues consequently saw her as someone who would be valuable if she didn't lose momentum before she ever really got going.

Jack, a new employee, was motivated and always up for a highly visible, challenging project. He consistently got the job done whether independently or on a team. Everyone thought Jack was a blast to work with on the big stuff. He seemed to be the newest rising star at his organization and expected to be promoted by year's end. After a few months, however, Jack's Achilles' Heel became evident. He never volunteered for minor behind-the-scenes tasks, and made excuses for why he couldn't do them. His coworkers routinely took turns, going to the Fedex office down the block and booking conference rooms for project meetings. Jack was only willing to do such things when others pressured him And even then, he complained so much that he gave others the impression that he thought he was too important to be bothered with the little stuff.

Celine was also a hard, but selective worker. She preferred conceptualizing projects more than implementing and following up. As a result, many of her most promising projects failed because she didn't proofread budgets before submitting them, keep track of interim deadlines, or document her creative process. Even when others told her that she needed to pay more attention to the little things, Celine continued in her usual manner. She rationalized to herself that she was a born visionary and didn't need to concern herself with the details. In this way, she sabotaged her chance to develop a professional identity.

Justin was an independent worker with very high standards. He preferred to complete tasks on his own, because that way he knew he'd get the job done right. When Justin had to work on a team, he pushed to divide the work up as soon as possible. He had a low tolerance for conflict, and he maintained as little contact with the other team members as possible. By isolating himself, he alienated the other team members and missed the opportunity to exchange valuable information with them. His actions often jeopardized the status of various projects, and earned him a reputation as a stubborn, rebellious loner.

Rayna always tried her hardest to do the right thing on the job. She was a team player who arrived early and stayed late every day. When she made a mistake, however, she rarely owned up to it immediately. She tried to hide the problem and hoped it would resolve itself. Occasionally, these issues did just go away. But most of the time they snowballed, creating other problems. In every case, Rayna then spent most of her day fearing that she would be discovered as the catalyst of the problems. Her performance suffered. Furthermore, what often started as a minor error with minimal consequences became a series of major problems that significantly impacted Rayna's organization.

Brad's fatal flaw as a professional presents a different spin on the fear-of-making-mistakes. He consistently met his job responsibilities, but he rarely exceeded them because that meant that he had to take calculated risks and stretch beyond the minimum requirements. He couldn't face the prospect of failing. By avoiding risks, Brad inhibited his career development both in the short and long term. Since he was reluctant to try new things, his skills remained stagnant and he stunted his career growth.

PROJECTING PROFESSIONALISM

Most of your private thoughts and feelings remain in your mind. But when it comes to your attitude about work, the way you act on the job will broadcast to the world what you're really thinking and feeling. In order for others to perceive you as a professional, you must behave in ways that show that you have the right attitude. Use the Smart Moves below to avoid the common mistakes that Monika, Jack, Celine, Justin, Rayna, and Brad made on the job.

Smart Move #19: Act Enthusiastic and Positive

Nobody likes working with a pessimist. But that doesn't mean you have to emulate the Energizer Bunny. You just need to show that you're an upbeat person who seeks to enjoy your job and do the best you can. Take the time to foster positive interactions with your coworkers. A friendly smile and occasional small talk about the weather, sports, vacations, and the like will go a long way towards building comfortable working relationships. When people feel that they know a little bit about you, it strengthens your ability to work better together. This is especially true if you can find some common interests that you share with those around you. Don't pretend to like classical music, miniature golf, and trekking in the Himaylas just because your coworker loves these things. But if you discover that you and your colleagues both enjoy, for example, horror movies, ethnic cooking, or playing soccer, you'll have something "safe" and engaging to chat about occasionally.

Positive Attitude Exercise

Directions: It's really important that you find ways that are genuine and easy to project a positive attitude on the job. In the space below, come up with seven ways that you can accomplish this, that fit with your style. They don't have to be big ways, just effective ones.

1.
2.
3.
4.
5.
6.
7.

Smart Move #20: Think Like an Owner or Top Dog

Approach your work as if you own your organization. This doesn't mean you should act cocky or try to make independent decisions that are over your head. It means that you should consistently generate initiatives that will help your organization achieve its mission. If you believe that you have as much to lose and gain as the CEO or executive director, you'll notice both details and big-picture trends that you never saw before. You'll make an ongoing, significant contribution by paying attention to things like cutting costs without sacrificing quality (see chapter 4, the bottom line section), developing new programs, designing on target marketing strategies, and selecting staff who are a good fit with the organization. Regardless of your actual level of responsibility, this mindset will enable you to show that you're invested in your organization.

Smart Move #21: Find Solutions to Problems

Your willingness to be a trouble-shooter is a key part of your attitude. Identifying problems isn't enough. You need to find creative, cost-effective solutions to these problems. It's valuable to find out what others have done in the past to deal with the same or similar issues. Sometimes an approach that worked before will work again. But don't automatically take the most obvious or familiar way just to resolve a problem quickly. First consider all of your options. When you're finished exploring your options, evaluate which one best fits the particular situation. You may come up with what is objectively the best solution for a problem. But before you run off to present it to your manager, stop and ask yourself if it's the most realistic solution. There are four main criteria to determine if your idea will fly. *Timing*: Is it timely, given your organization's other priorities? *Cost:* Is it cost-effective, given what it adds to or saves from the bottom line? *Politics:* Will it be well received, given the politics of the situation? Who will be directly and indirectly affected by your proposed change? Who should you present your idea to? How should you present it? *Culture:* Given your organization's culture, how radical a change are you proposing? At what pace are you proposing to implement this change?

Trouble-Shooting Exercise

Directions: Write down a problem you've encountered on the job. Then try to come up with as many ways as possible to solve it—even if they initially sound unrealistic or silly. You can include the actual way that you approached the problem when it happened in your list of possibilities. Next, try to modify each possible solution to make it fit the problem. This may mean reworking it or combining one or more solutions into a new solution. Narrow down the revised list of options to your top three. Then decide which one is the best approach and why.

Step 1—Concisely describe the problem

Step 2—Brainstorm possible solutions

Step 3—Modify your solutions

Step 4—Pick your top three solutions

Step 5—Select the best approach and the rationale for it

Smart Move #22: Do Grunt Work With a Smile

Along these lines, you have to demonstrate that you're willing to do grunt work. Rising to the challenge of big, highly visible projects will help establish your competency. Every job involves some small, often mundane tasks. If you take on these responsibilities without grumbling, you'll come across as a team player instead of as an egomaniac or a snob.

Grunt Work Exercise

Directions: In order to demonstrate your willingness to do grunt work, you need to know where it's hiding in your everyday or periodic, project-based responsibilities. Then you can focus on when you've done it and when you've avoided doing it and why. In the cases where you've avoided it, document what the consequences have been.

Example #1 Done It:	Example #2 Done It:	Example #3 Done It:
_____	_____	_____
_____	_____	_____
_____	_____	_____

Example #1 Didn't Do It/ Why Not/ Consequences:	Example #2 Didn't Do It/ Why Not/ Consequences:	Example #3 Didn't Do It/ Why Not/ Consequences:
_____	_____	_____
_____	_____	_____
_____	_____	_____

Smart Move #23: Be Detail Oriented

From entry level to executive positions, details can make or break your career. You can develop the most creative, groundbreaking ideas your organization has ever encountered. But if you don't tie up the loose ends, you won't be able to implement any of them. And you'll continually sabotage your efforts. After all, what good is a proposal for a stellar project if the budget numbers are wrong? How can you ever complete projects on time if you ignore the deadlines? How can you hand off a project to someone else if you don't accurately document your work?

Smart Move #24: Play for the Team

Although *being a team player* is an overused expression, it's more important than ever to be one. Increasingly, you're likely to work for an organization that will expect you to work in a variety of team situations. You'll work with both your immediate colleagues and those in other areas to complete projects. Some of these projects may last for several weeks, a few months, or even a couple of years. You may even work with more than one team at the same time. On an informal basis, others may ask for your help to meet a deadline, to get advice about a problem, to serve on an interdepartmental committee, or to learn a new skill. Actively pitch in and assist your colleagues, because it's the professional thing to do. This will also help to create a more stimulating, cooperative workplace. Even if you don't know for sure when, know that someday you'll need to turn to those colleagues for help.

Some people shy away from working on teams because of the potential for conflict. Both you and your team members may have to adapt your natural working styles to work harmoniously. As we mentioned in the Introduction, there are many different motivational, learning, and decision-making styles. You can't control or change others' styles. But you can become aware enough of your own style that you can blend it with the others' styles. Ask yourself questions such as: What is my primary motivation in a team setting—maintaining calm working relationships, getting my ideas accepted, establishing a leadership position, or something else? How do I learn best and how can I apply this process to understanding others' points of view? How do I usually communicate with others and why am I usually misunderstood (e.g., my requests sound like demands because I am so direct)? Do I make decisions quickly or slowly? Do I need to first listen to all of the information or respond to others' comments immediately, talking issues through out loud as they arise?

Teamwork Exercise

Directions: In the space below think of at least six ways that you can develop your teamwork skills. Try to come up with two activities from each category: formal, on-the-job activities (related to current and prospective projects); informal, on-the-job activities (e.g., planning a holiday party, organizing a company softball team, participating in a company-sponsored mentoring program, etc.); and outside activities (volunteer work, social groups, cultural activities, hobbies, etc.).

Formal, On-the-Job Activities

Your Prospective Role

1.

2.

Informal, On-the-Job Activities

Your Prospective Role

1.

2.

Outside-of-Work Activities

Your Prospective Role

1.

2.

Smart Move #25: Admit Your Mistakes and Limits

Part of the spirit of teamwork requires that you admit your mistakes and take responsibility for them when they occur. Many people are afraid that if they point out their errors, they'll get into more trouble than if they hide them. However in most cases, buried mistakes surface at a later time. Hiding mistakes may trigger other problems.

Everyone makes mistakes—you'll earn the respect of others more readily by owning up to yours and fixing them as quickly as possible. Depending on the severity of an error, this may be an uncomfortable thing to do. Pretending a problem doesn't exist, though, will also probably make you worry about being discovered. This concern, coupled with the real damage that the problem causes, drains you of valuable energy and time. Conserve your resources by admitting mistakes, learning from them, and avoiding repeating them.

Note that one of the most common causes of mistakes is people's attempts to hide their limits. Instead of admitting when they don't know how to do something, or need help, some people just plow ahead stubbornly. Everyone has limits. One of the hallmarks of professionals at all stages of their careers is that they know their limits concerning knowledge, skills, and their ability to get work done. True professionals are forthright about these things and give themselves a chance to grow.

Mistakes Exercise

Directions: Think of two examples of mistakes you've made on the job, including the context in which each happened. Briefly describe what you've done to remedy each of them and how long after you've realized the mistake you took action to address it. Document the outcome of your action and its timing. Consider what alternative action and/or timing, if any, may have been more effective in each instance.

Mistake #1: _____

When It Happened:

The Circumstances Surrounding the Mistake:

Action You Took:

How Long After You Realized the Mistake You Took Action:

Outcome of Your Action Itself and the Timing:

Alternative Action and/or Timing:

Mistake #2: _____

When It Happened:

The Circumstances Surrounding the Mistake:

Action You Took:

How Long After You Realized the Mistake You Took Action:

Outcome of Your Action Itself and the Timing:

Alternative Action and/or Timing:

Smart Move #26: Take Calculated Risks

Every outstanding professional takes smart risks from time to time. Some appropriate risks may be reaching out to build a business relationship with a difficult colleague, taking on an assignment in a different location, or spending some extra time working on an alternative approach to a project. There's no guarantee that such risks will work out, but they'll pay off in terms of letting others know that you're someone who takes initiative. This ability will make you a valued employee and it will help you to exceed, not just meet, your job requirements. Your manager expects you to excel whenever possible, and will measure your performance against her highest standards (see chapter 3). You can't do everything perfectly, so focus on calculated risks that match your manager's priorities. If you're continually setting new goals to grow professionally, you'll always face new learning curves. As long as you make both a good faith effort and steady progress towards these new goals, you'll stay on your manager's good side.

Risk-Taking Exercise

Directions: Take a few minutes to think of three calculated risks that you might want to take in your current position. Then briefly evaluate the pros and cons of taking each risk. Even if you don't actually take these particular risks, it will give you practice in generating and evaluating possibilities on an ongoing basis.

Risk #1:

Pros:

Cons:

Risk #2:

Pros:

Cons:

Risk #3:

Pros:

Cons:

Smart Move #27: Incorporate Other Aspects of Attitude

So now you're primed to be a positive-approaching, owner-thinking, problem-solving, grunt-working, detail-oriented, team-playing, mistake- and limit-admitting, and risk-taking worker. As if all of these approaches weren't enough to constitute a professional attitude, there are also other Smart Moves that are integral parts of your attitude. For example, we talk about being an active listener in the chapter 1 clients section. We explain managing your emotions in the chapter 2 expectations section. We discuss developing a self-managing philosophy in the chapter 3 responsibility section. And we reinforce becoming a lifelong learner in the chapter 4 hot competencies section.

PROTOCOL

CHALLENGE: DEALING WITH PHONE CALLS, E-MAILS, PRESENTATIONS, MEETINGS, AND PUBLIC PLACES

Zach picked up the phone, mumbled "Yes," and went back to munching on his sandwich while clicking his computer keyboard. He sounded distracted and uninterested in what the caller had to say. The caller asked Zach if there was a better time for him to talk. Speaking very rapidly, Zach told the caller that now was fine. The caller continued explaining the problem and Zach responded with occasional, distracted "uh-huhs" and "hmms." The caller became exasperated and ended the phone conversation abruptly. Zach assumed it was because the caller was having a bad day. Unaware that he'd done anything wrong, Zach was relieved to be done with the call. He returned to focusing on his work and lunch. Several months later, Zach was shocked that his manager gave him the lowest possible rating in the verbal communication and responsiveness categories of his performance review. He specifically pointed to his phone behavior as a major source of the problem.

Mitch hated using e-mail, but because it was a popular method of communication at his organization he was forced to use it. He frequently did not receive critical information by deadlines and often neglected to give people answers to their questions when they wanted them. He'd protest that he'd sent e-mails requesting or providing such information on time, but the recipients hadn't checked their e-mail messages until it was too late. Also, Mitch's colleagues often told him that they weren't sure how to interpret the tone of his e-mails. They couldn't decipher when he was kidding around or being serious, and therefore often got offended or misunderstood his intent. As if these hazards weren't bad enough, Mitch once sent an e-mail congratulating an award winner to all of the nominees. He didn't realize his mistake until they all showed up for the awards' lunch the following day. He also inadvertently deleted all of his correspondence about the awards program, which was the only documentation about the process. The final blow was when Mitch complained about his manager in an e-mail to a friend. Mitch's system crashed and he had to ask for help from the computer support group. The person who fixed Mitch's computer saw the e-mail and told Mitch's manager.

Jenna was excited and scared about making her first big presentation at work. She had waited until the day before the presentation to prepare, but she felt confident that the purpose and scope were well defined. She arrived at the small auditorium about fifteen minutes before the start time. About half of the twenty-five audience members had already arrived. She put her notes on the podium. Suddenly, she felt a run in her pantyhose. Glancing at her watch, she realized she didn't have time to change them. So, Jenna attempted to hide her leg behind the podium. Jenna then realized that her throat was very dry, but she didn't have any water. By this point, Jenna was a nervous wreck. It was time to start her presentation, so she took a deep breath and buried her face in her notes. When she was through, she looked up and noticed from the clock on the wall that she had made it through a ten-minute presentation in four minutes.

Trish rushed through the conference room door just as a meeting was about to begin. She scanned the room for a seat and spotted the only empty chair—at the side of the moderator. She quickly slipped into her seat and realized that she didn't have anything to write with, or her copy of the meeting agenda. She quietly asked her coworker, Roger, if she could borrow a pen and share his agenda. Roger, a notorious big-mouth, replied loudly, "Sure Trish, here's a pen and you can look on with me." Trish wished that she had gotten to the meeting a little earlier so that she could have sat next to someone else. Throughout the meeting, the moderator asked the participants if they had any questions. But Trish had a hard time getting noticed, since she was out of the moderator's direct line of vision. Getting increasingly frustrated, she repeatedly brought up points out of the sequence of the agenda. She also jumped into the discussion whenever she could with strong, opposing reactions to others' perspectives. Sometimes, Trish conceded that someone else had a good idea. But, despite her supportive words and tone of voice, her body language sent a different message to the group. She rarely made eye contact with the person she addressed, leaned way back in her chair, and crossed her arms in front of her. As a result, the other attendees didn't really believe that Trish meant what she said.

Kyle typically watched what he said (and to whom) in formal work settings, such as in meetings or on the phone, and at other times let his professional guard down. When he rode the elevator, ate lunch in the cafeteria, and attended holiday parties, he and his coworkers freely talked about both the good and the bad stuff going on in their work lives. Kyle and his coworkers all got passed over for promotions that year. Others who were not as talented as them moved ahead, and Kyle wondered why this was. He found out that their lack of professional demeanor in public places had held them back; their superiors had gotten wind of some of the things Kyle and his buddies had been saying. Kyle and his coworkers tried to explain that their jokes, frustrations, and updates had been misconstrued. Like a game of telephone, others had overheard things out of context and misrepresented what they really meant. But, even so, the senior managers questioned Kyle and his friends' judgment and decided that they were not high-caliber professionals.

Perfecting Your Schtick

Since you spend so much time at work and share so many resources with your colleagues, you need to be aware of the common, formal situations that require correct protocol. In the rest of this section we'll address five situations that most people encounter frequently: phone calls, e-mail, presentations, meetings, and public places. The Smart Moves that follow are important, because they show you how to avoid making the mistakes that Zach, Mitch, Jenna, Trish, and Kyle made.

Smart Move #28: Give The Caller Your Undivided Attention

Since you never know who may be calling (unless you have a caller ID), it's in your best interest to approach a phone call as if it's the most important thing in the universe at that moment.

Smart Move #29: Be Consistent and Sincere When Answering The Phone

When you answer your phone, make sure you remember that you're at work and use whatever phrase is acceptable at your organization. It may be just saying your full name, or a variation of this such as: "Joe Bloggs. How may I help you?"; "ABC Department. This is Joe. How may I help you?"; or "XYZ Company. Joe speaking." All of us screw up once in a while and think we're at home, answering the phone, "Hello?" When this happens, just recover and add your usual opening line.

Smart Move #30: Identify Yourself and Your Purpose Up Front When Calling

When you place a call, make sure you identify yourself by name and affiliation up front, if necessary. This prevents the caller from having to guess your identity and saves them from feeling embarrassed or aggravated. Also, state the purpose for the call after you identify yourself: "I'm calling to let you know that . . ." or "I'm calling because I need some input into. . . ."

Smart Move #31: Monitor Your Tone of Voice

You may be deep in thought or working under a tight deadline. But sounding spacey or tense isn't the way to go on the phone. Whether you really need to speak with someone or the phone ringing interrupts you, take a deep breath to clear your head and speak in a calm, directed tone.

Smart Move #32: Pace Yourself During a Phone Call

Similarly, the speed of your speech may vary depending on your personality or mood. Speaking too quickly is particularly common. You naturally may be a fast talker or start racing when you're uptight. Either way, slow it down. If the other person can't understand you the first time, you'll have to repeat yourself anyway. It's especially important to be sensitive to pacing your speech when talking with people who are in different parts of the country or world. Regional speech patterns vary greatly and you need to adjust to them—by talking faster or slower—without sounding patronizing.

Smart Move #33: Periodically Summarize What You Hear

As we mentioned in the previous section, be an active listener (see the clients section in chapter 1). Whether you initiate or receive a call, it's important to clarify that you understand what the other person is saying. You can do this by periodically summarizing the key points of the conversation . Begin such summaries with phrases like, "So what I hear you saying is that you need . . ." or "It sounds like you're concerned about. . . ." The caller will either affirm or correct what you've said. Then you can proceed with what to do about it.

Smart Move #34: Take Responsibility for Understanding
Different Speech Styles

If you're having a lot of trouble understanding what someone is saying because their accent or manner of speaking is different from yours, try your best to be gracious about it. Be patient and take responsibility for clarifying the other person's meaning by summarizing. Sometimes you may just not get it at all. Then it's okay to politely ask someone to repeat themselves by saying something like, "I'm sorry. I didn't understand that last sentence. Would you mind repeating it?"

In some cases, meeting with someone in person will help you understand what they're saying more easily. If it's convenient, suggest that you stop by their desk to talk about the issue in person for a few minutes. If they're far away, suggest that you call them back and invite a colleague who would be relevant to join the conversation. Select someone who may be able to help you understand the conversation more readily.

Smart Move #35: Take Notes During a Phone Conversation

Notes will help you remember key information and make it easier to follow up later. These notes also provide you with a record of what was agreed to during the discussion. If someone creates a problem for you down the road, you'll have proof of what really happened. You can also use these phone notes to chart the evolution of a project and streamline the process the next time. You'll learn about your phone habits, including how much time you're actually spending on the phone every day or during the course of a specific project.

Smart Move #36: Leave a Specific Phone Message

When you need to leave a message for someone, make it as specific a message as possible. That way you may save both you and the caller an extra phone call. Sometimes you're calling about a time-sensitive and/or confidential matter. And you may reach someone's voice mail or their assistant. Make the most out of your message by clearly leaving your name, phone number, times you'll be available, and enough information to indicate why you're calling. Don't cry wolf. Differentiate between something that can wait and an urgent matter. In other cases, you may need non-confidential information that the caller can locate and send or give to you. By letting them know what's up in your message, they can return your call with the information in hand. Or they can refer you to the right party, especially if they reach your voice mail. Then you've saved an unnecessary game of phone tag.

Smart Move #37: Treat a Conference Call Like an In-Person Meeting

Conference calls require unique protocol. They're a practical, time-saving way to communicate with more than one person at a time. Act as you would in a face-to-face meeting. Be prepared with your calendar in front of you as well as any information that may be relevant to the call. The coordinator of the call should introduce everyone at the beginning and state the purpose and projected length of the call. Defer to those in a position of power when appropriate. Don't interrupt someone else when they're speaking. And take good notes since lots of information will be discussed from many different perspectives.

From time to time, make your presence known by acknowledging what someone else is saying. But don't just repeat what that person is saying or compete for center stage. Also, don't fall into the trap of getting too casual, even if you know everyone involved, remember that it's still a business meeting and, not a personal call.

Consider everyone's personal style and balance yours with theirs as much as possible. This can be challenging, since there are more than two people involved. When in doubt, follow the lead of the moderator or the most senior person on the call.

Smart Move #38: Assess Your Phone Call Skills

Phone Call Exercise

Directions: Put a check next to any phone skills below that you believe you're proficient at. Put an X next to any skills that you need to work on. Then make it a point to work on at least one new skill each day. Review the entire checklist from time to time to ensure that you maintain and improve the full range of skills that are part of phone protocol.

Making/Receiving Regular Phone Calls

_____ Opening remarks

_____ Tone of voice

_____ Pace of speech

_____ Active listening

_____ Resolving miscommunications

_____ Note taking

Leaving Messages

_____ Speaking clearly

_____ Stating your full name (and spelling if necessary)

_____ Clarifying the purpose of the call

_____ Indicating the relative importance of the call

_____ Giving the best times to reach you

Conference Calls

_____ Having your calendar accessible

_____ Not interrupting others

_____ Taking notes

_____ Acknowledging others' comments

_____ Maintaining a professional demeanor

Smart Move #39: Time E-mails Right

Don't count on your e-mails being read soon after you send them. Some people choose to read their e-mails less frequently than others. This may mean that your e-mail will sit around for hours or even over night. So it's important to time them right. And if a message is really important, but off schedule, then consider sending it another way. Sometimes inter-office mail or voice mail is more efficient.

Smart Move #40: Tune E-mails Up

It's easy to slip into the habit of writing e-mails in a more casual style than you would write a memo or other document. This is especially true if you have a personal e-mail account at home. Depending on your organization, it's probably okay to make your e-mail messages more brief and less formal than you would other written communications. But be careful about using abbreviations. For example, if your account name doesn't have your full name in it and you end your message with just your initials, the recipient may confuse you with someone else. Watch expressions of emotion such as "<sigh>." Comments like this as are extraneous, unless you're sending someone a play or movie script. Ditto for cutesy symbols, such as smiley faces made with a colon and right parenthesis. These extras are inappropriate and diminish your professional credibility.

Smart Move #41: Send E-mails Carefully

If you've ever inadvertently sent an e-mail to the wrong address, you know how this can be one of the top ten most embarrassing situations of your career. The ease of sending e-mail is great, when you do it right. But when you goof, you wish it weren't quite so easy. You may accidentally send an e-mail meant for one or two people's eyes only to an entire distribution list. Naturally, some e-mails are no big deal. You just feel stupid for sending it to the wrong address. Other e-mails are highly confidential. Generally, it's not a good idea to send this kind of information via e-mail, just in case.

Smart Move #42: Print E-mails Before You Delete Them

One of the biggest letdowns related to e-mail is when you delete an entire record of a project or correspondence by accident. Sometimes you can get delete-key happy when you're cleaning your files. Simply avoid this problem by printing out your e-mail messages every time you send or receive them. In certain e-mail systems you can also save an e-mail as a word processing document on your hard drive. Either way, you can decide to purge your files later. In the meantime, you're covered just in case you need a particular document.

Smart Move #43: Keep Your Professional Guard Up in E-mails

Since e-mail systems are the property of an organization, your confidentiality isn't guaranteed. Managers and computer support people have access to your files. So don't gossip, complain, belittle, or conduct personal business through your work e-mail account. If you do any of these things, you may end up derailing your career.

Smart Move #44: Start Preparing Presentations ASAP

Occasionally, you'll only have a day or a few hours to prepare for a presentation. That's not a problem if you're recycling one that you've done many times before. Otherwise, you need to give yourself as much lead time as you can, to ensure that you end up with a high-quality presentation.

Smart Move #45: Establish the Why and the What of Presentations

First you need to get clear about why you're doing the presentation and the scope of the material you should cover. If you sail ahead with only a vague idea in your mind, it will be difficult to complete. And your presentation will likely be too broad. When in doubt, ask your manager for clarification about the why and what of your presentation. Don't let your ego get in the way. It's more embarrassing and damaging to your reputation if you flub it than if you ask for guidance up front and nail it.

Smart Move #46: Identify Each Presentation's Audience

Knowing your audience will further enable you to target the format and content of your presentation. Presenting an orientation program to forty new hires of different levels is much different than welcoming ten senior managers who've just relocated from overseas. The two audiences need different amounts of information about your organization presented in different ways.

Smart Move #47: Arrange the Right Place for Presentations

Where you host your presentation matters as much as its quality. Gear your location toward the size of your audience. Ten people will feel lost in an auditorium, while thirty people may feel too crowded in a small conference room. Also, make sure that the space you choose can accommodate the format of the program. For example, if you plan to give audience members interactive exercises that require writing, they will need desks or tables to write on. Any special equipment is another consideration. Microphones, tape players, slides, and the like must fit and work properly.

Smart Move #48: Organize Your Presentation's Content

There are many different types of presentations, such as interactive training seminars on a specialized topic like teamwork, organization-wide quarterlies to report on the organization's performance, new hire orientations, and department staff meeting show-and-tells. Each presentation will vary in terms of the content and format. In all of these scenarios, you can follow this basic sequence of five steps to make your presentation clear and engaging:

1. **Use a Hook:** After introducing yourself (if necessary), begin your presentation with a hook that grabs the audience's attention and makes them want to hear more. You can cite a relevant quote, tell an appropriate joke, give an interesting fact related to the topic, or tell a brief anecdote.

2. **Review the Agenda:** Tell the audience what you're going to cover during the presentation, in chronological order. If you're giving a long presentation, you may want to mention when the breaks will happen. Some people also like to pass out handouts at the beginning of a presentation. For example, you can provide copies of the agenda, a list of slides, or a detailed outline of your presentation. Other presenters opt to hand out relevant material, such as written exercises, right before they do them. Still others choose to pass out handouts—such as outlines—at the end of the presentation for the audience to take home. One reason some presenters don't distribute handouts at the beginning is that they don't want the audience getting distracted by reading ahead. Another reason is that some handouts are only supplemental resources, such as reading lists, contact people, or places to visit for more information.

3. **Illustrate Your Key Points:** Use concrete, vivid examples to help the audience understand what you're saying. Again, consider your audience by selecting examples that they can relate to. Don't use boating metaphors when addressing a group of pilots, carpentry analogies when speaking to a group of teachers, or military analogies when presenting to a group of human rights lobbyists. Take the obvious route and draw from your audience's field of interest to make a point come alive. Also, you may get a group's attention by making them mad, like in the previous situation. But then your audience won't necessarily be receptive to what you have to say.

4. Summarize the Presentation: At the end of the presentation, review the highlights and themes. This way you can reinforce and synthesize what you want the audience to learn and remember afterwards.

5. Allow Time for Questions: There are several ways to deal with questions. You can take questions randomly throughout the presentation, you can field them periodically after each section, or you can ask the audience to hold their questions until the end. The most important thing is that you leave room for people to clarify and further explore what you're presenting.

Smart Move #49: Practice Presentations Before You Speak

You may be tempted to do a presentation by either winging it or memorizing a script. The best way to prepare, however, is to familiarize yourself without your material. Review what you want to say and make notes with key phrases on cue cards or slides. This way you can use a conversational tone, rather than sounding stiff or overly rehearsed.

Also, you'll be able to make eye contact with the audience if you don't read directly from your notes. After all, no one wants to stare at the top or back of your head the whole time. While you speak, scan the room. If you're uncomfortable making direct eye contact focus on the spot between people's eyebrows above the bridge of their noses. They won't know the difference. And keep scanning. This will make everyone feel included.

Speak clearly by projecting your voice to an appropriate level and enunciating your words. Remember, too, that you don't have to fill every silence. Pausing for air, for emphasis, or to let a point sink in is acceptable. Filling these moments with excessive "umm's" or "uhh's" is annoying to a listener and detracts from your credibility as a speaker. Pace yourself. You don't want to break into the *Guinness Book of World Records* as the fastest presenter or as the presenter whose audience fell asleep from the excruciatingly slow pace.

Smart Move #50: Plan Your Appearance for Presentations

Match your outfit to the occasion. Whatever will give you the most credibility with the audience is the way to go. Even if you work at an organization where people dress informally or it's casual Friday, make sure that you dress appropriately. Since you're the presenter, you probably need to dress one level up from what everyone else is wearing. If your audience is already formally dressed, dress accordingly but sharper than usual. Make sure to set aside your outfit for the big day. Opening up your closet to discover that what you wanted to wear is at the dry cleaner will just raise your stress level.

You never know what may happen on the day of a presentation. Pantyhose rip, ties get stained, buttons fall off garments, and hair accessories get lost. It's smart to bring extra clothes to avoid hassles like these.

Right before the presentation, double check your appearance. Fix your hair, check your teeth, and straighten your clothes. This will give you the confidence to go out there and concentrate 100 percent on your presentation. And this will help your audience focus on what you're saying, not on the spinach that's caught between your front teeth.

Smart Move #51: Tie Up Loose Ends Before Presentations

Arrive at your presentation site early to make sure it's set up properly. See if everything is in place and working, including: chairs, tables, microphones, audiovisual equipment, lights, temperature, refreshments, paper, and pencils. Give yourself more than fifteen minutes to do this. As we mentioned above, you need time to check your appearance as well as the room arrangement. And you don't want to be doing these things while your audience is arriving.

Smart Move #52: Be Ready for Anything at Meetings

You'll probably attend meetings at least once in a while. These may take place in someone's office, in a conference room, auditorium, or outside of the office. They may be staff meetings, team project meetings, or outside client meetings. Regardless of where and why you're meeting, it's important to prepare beforehand. Bring any necessary materials and information you need to fully participate.

Smart Move #53: Sit in the Right Spot at Meetings

Arrive a few minutes early so you can settle in and get a handle on the layout of the room. Seat yourself across or in the direct line of vision of the facilitator. This will enable you to become fully engaged and noticed in the meeting. Be aware of who you sit next to on either side. In a larger meeting, you'll probably sit with your manager and department members. Try to position yourself next to others with good reputations. This will further enhance your image.

Smart Move #54: Listen and Think, Then Speak at Meetings

Strike a balance between speaking and listening during a meeting. It's more important to make thoughtful, concise contributions than to speak excessively without saying anything substantial. Others will respect and listen to you, both then and in the future. When you do speak, try to tie in what you're saying with what others have said—regardless of whether you agree. Think before you speak; during a particularly volatile meeting, some people will react impulsively and say things that they later wish they could take back.

Smart Move #55: Stay Focused on Each Meeting's Agenda

It's primarily the moderator's responsibility to keep the meeting agenda on track. You can be a constructive participant by thinking before talking. Consider whether what you have to say is relevant and help to steer the conversation when it gets wildly off topic. Ask the group to clarify the meeting's goal, or politely suggest that you get back to the agenda. These are both good ways to keep things moving forward.

Smart Move #56: Monitor Your Body Language at Meetings

Your body language will also help you get your points across during meetings. Regardless of how courteous your words and tone of voice are, the signals that you send by how you hold your body need to match. For example, saying that you're excited about a particular idea or willing to help isn't enough if you're slumped down in your chair with your arms crossed in front of your chest. Noticeably tapping your foot, drumming your fingers, biting your nails, frowning, staring up at the ceiling or down at the floor for long periods of time, or visibly doodling also may send the message to others that you don't care or don't have your act together. Leaning forward slightly in your chair, making direct eye contact with the current speaker, and making your facial expressions match your words are all simple ways to show your interest and sincerity.

Smart Move #57: Take Solid Meeting Notes

You may think you'll remember what went on, but it's easy to get caught up in the whirlwind of a busy day and forget important details. Jotting down even a few key points will help refresh your memory later. This will make it easier when you have to share the content of a meeting with others or when you need to follow up on matters decided during the meeting. After a meeting is over, review your notes for follow-up steps. Transfer these steps into your organizer, calendar, and/or project plan. Then file these notes in an accessible place. If the meeting is a staff meeting, you can create a staff meetings folder. If it was a project meeting, then it's a good idea to have a file specifically related to the particular project. Doing your filing as soon as possible will prevent it from building up. No one likes to face the boring and tedious prospect of sorting and filing a tower of paper at the end of a week or month. Shoving your notes in a drawer or a miscellaneous file may put them out of sight for a little while. But you'll eventually need them and have to wade through lots of other unrelated stuff to locate them.

Finally, evaluate how the outcome of the meeting affects your current projects and priorities. If you need to, ask your manager to help you juggle your work load if any new commitments have arisen during the meeting.

Smart Move #58: Assess Your Meeting Skills

Meetings Exercise

Put a check next to any meeting skills below that you believe you're proficient at. Put an X next to any skills that you need to work on. Make it a point to work on at least one new skill each day. Review the entire checklist from time to time to ensure that you maintain and improve the full range of skills that are important to meetings protocol.

Before a Meeting

_____ Bringing relevant materials

_____ Arriving early

_____ Seating yourself strategically

During a Meeting

_____ Balancing listening and talking

_____ Tying in what you say with others' comments

_____ Helping keep the meeting on track

_____ Monitoring your body language

_____ Taking good notes

After a Meeting

_____ Reviewing your notes for follow-up steps

_____ Filing your notes immediately

_____ Evaluating how the meeting affects your projects and priorities

Smart Move #59: Locate Danger Zones in Public Places

During the course of your workday, you may consider your time in public places to be down time. In reality, elevators, restrooms, cafeterias, lobbies, outside areas near the building, commuter transportation (buses, subways, ferries, and trains), and work-related special events (holiday parties, staff retreats, and birthday celebrations) are hidden danger zones for letting your professional guard down.

Smart Move #60: Keep it Simple in Public Places

It may be fun to catch up on the latest happenings at work or in your personal life with friends. But it's important to be aware of who's around you. You never know who may overhear what you're saying. Whether they misunderstand what they hear and take it out of context or not, they may possibly repeat it to others and damage your reputation. The safest approach is to only make small talk in public places. Save your venting or questionable jokes for after hours in your personal life. And encourage your friends to do the same.

Smart Move #61: Maintain Your Composure at Celebrations

At special events, take advantage of these opportunities to get to know your colleagues in a friendly environment. Never forget to maintain your professional sensibility. Don't drink too much (if any) alcohol, don't make off-the-cuff remarks about what others are wearing or doing, and don't act in ways that draw unwanted attention to yourself. Sometimes you may not want to, but must attend such events. In these instances, make a brief appearance and then leave.

Smart Move #62: Assess Your Public Places and Special Events Skills

Public Places/Special Events Exercise

Directions: Put a check next to any public places skills below that you believe you're proficient at. Put an X next to any skills that you need to work on. Then make it a point to work on at least one new skill each day. Review the entire checklist from time to time to ensure that you maintain and improve the full range of skills that are important to public places/special events protocol.

Public Places

_____ Identifying public places that are danger zones

_____ Being aware of who's around you

_____ Making only small talk

_____ Encouraging others to make only small talk

Special Events

_____ Identifying special events that are danger zones

_____ Setting limits on casualness

_____ Monitoring your drinking

_____ Attending for the right amount of time

**Phoning, E-mailing, Presenting, Meeting, and
Socializing Your Way Out Of A Job**

1) Always let people know that your messages are urgent—even when they aren't.
2) Start an underground gossip swap through your work e-mail account about your colleagues.
3) Work on your big presentation for the first time the night before.
4) Sit next to the loudest mouth colleague at every meeting so no one will notice you.
5) Pursue your secret ambition to be a political cartoonist by using meetings to draw caricatures of the participants.
6) Pig out at all social events. After all, it's free food!
7) Play twenty questions—the personal life version—to get to know the bigwigs at your holiday party.

CLOTHES

CHALLENGE: DECIDING WHAT TO WEAR

Michael arrived for his first day of work in the suit he wore to his first interview. He figured that he'd make a good impression by dressing up as much as possible. But after a few minutes, he noticed that everyone around him was dressed in more casual, sporty clothes. As the day progressed, he felt increasingly self-conscious about his clothes and acted more like a visitor than a new employee. Since he spent most of his day worrying about sticking out rather than learning how to fit in, Michael ended the day just as clueless as when he began.

Before Sarah even started her new job, she decided that fitting in wasn't important. She showed up for her first few weeks at work in her casual, weekend clothes. Everyone around her wore casual, but professional clothes. Determined to work hard, Sarah figured that her outstanding contributions should ensure her career success. But her manager repeatedly approached her about upgrading her work wardrobe. Sarah told him that she was more comfortable and generated better work when she wore casual clothes. Her manager responded that he expected her to comply with the dress standards of the organization. He also said that, within reason, he was happy to accommodate her and the other department members' individual work style preferences. But this flexibility didn't extend to "dressing down."

DRESSING THE PART

What you wear will affect the way in which others perceive you on the job. Whether you dress up too much like Michael, or dress down too much like Sarah, what you wear sends a message to your colleagues about how well you fit in. Others, especially those in positions of power, will interpret your choice of dress as a reflection of your level of commitment to your career and to the organization. Working hard isn't enough. You need to pay as much attention to your wardrobe as you do to the quality of your work.

Smart Move #63: Observe Others

Whether it's your first or fourth job, it's hard to get the hang of a new situation. Getting dressed in the morning shouldn't have to be a hassle. Your organization may or may not have a formal dress code. If it doesn't, you can eliminate the guessing game by observing what your peers are wearing every day. It's a good idea to check this out before you begin working so you can show up on your first day ready to go.

Once you have a handle on what the typical dress is at your workplace, don't go on a shopping spree right away. First, check out what you have in your closet. Do some rearranging. Put all the things that you could wear to work on one side of the closet and see how much you've really got. You may be surprised to discover that you've got more appropriate clothes than you think. Then supplement your wardrobe gradually. As you consider what you have and what you need, remember that everything you wear counts. Accessories matter as much as your basic outfit. So be careful to coordinate ties, jewelry, shoes, and other items to complete the look.

Smart Move #64: Take an Inventory of Your Closet

Clothes Exercise

Directions: List all work wardrobe items that you can think of that you may need. Then take inventory of your closet. In the "Have" column, put a "Y" next to all items that you currently own that are in usable condition and next to items that you have but need more of (e.g., ties, pantyhose, etc.). Put an "N" next to items that you don't yet own but also need. In the "Need" column, put a * next to all items that you need more of or need at all. Next, in the "Priority Ranking" column, put a ranking next to each of the items that you need. Try to be realistic about what you need versus what you want. Finally, jot down some store names and approximate costs of each item you need to buy.

Item Name	Have Y/N	Need (*)	Priority Ranking 1= urgent, 2= important, 3= can wait	Options Where to Buy Store Names, $
1.				
2.				
3.				
4.				
5.				
6.				
7.				
8.				

Smart Move #65: Dress for the Occasion

There will be times when you have to adjust your clothes to fit the occasion. For example, many organizations have instituted casual Fridays or casual wear in the summer. The good news is that many retail clothing stores now stock casual work clothes in a range of prices—from more expensive to affordable. But casual still means different things at different places. Always pay attention to what's the right thing to do at your workplace.

There may be days when you have contact with outside clients or internal meetings and presentations. These occasions will require you to upgrade your attire. You can check with your manager and peers to coordinate what's appropriate in each case. Taking the extra step to look good on these days will help you feel confident as well as enhance your reputation as a team player and committed employee.

Smart Move #66: Show Your Desire to Advance Your Career

To get ahead, it's important to strike a balance between fitting in with your peers and dressing for the job you want next. You don't have to alienate your contemporaries or spend a fortune on your wardrobe. Subtly dressing a little more professionally than your current level will make a good impression on your superiors. They'll recognize your attention to your appearance and begin thinking of you as a potential candidate for promotion.

Smart Move #67: Be as Individualistic as Your Workplace

Many of you may wonder how to express your sense of style without getting fired. One way to address this problem is to insert your personal style into your daily attire on a small scale. Wear a piece of jewelry, such as a watch with a funky face, or a striking accessory that can be removed if necessary during the day. This approach will enable you to feel like yourself without attracting unwanted attention. If you want to make a bigger statement, then consider the potential consequences before you act. For example, if you're an investment banker, wearing a tie with cartoon characters or a really off beat pin may elicit some negative comments about your professionalism. On the other hand, if you're an assistant to a cutting edge fashion designer, wearing something individualistic will help you fit right in.

Smart Move #68: Take the Dress Blues as a Signal

During your career, what you have to wear every day will probably influence how happy you are in your field, your job, and at a specific organization. Some people feel like they're in a straight jacket when wearing a suit, while others can't perform optimally in jeans. So when you consider the ideal environment for your professional development, remember to take into account what you'll be wearing most days. Even in the same field, this may vary widely from organization to organization. You may be able to wear one thing in a particular position, but need to change your attire for another job at the same organization.

Suddenly feeling uncomfortable with the required wardrobe in your current job may be a signal that something deeper is wrong with your career situation. It's then time to reconsider what the real issues are for you at that point in time. What's missing for you? Collegiality, competition, structure, freedom, or something else? Let your reactions to your dress code guide you about what you need to do next to best manage your career. It's possible that you're ready for a change. After all, it's common for all of our needs to change over time. It may have been fine—or even fun—for you to dress one way at work at the beginning of your career. But even one or two years later, you may realize that you want to work in a different kind of environment (see chapter 6 for help on figuring out exactly what's wrong with your current career).

You Know You're Not Dressing for Success When ...

...you dress up when up everyone else dresses down;

...you open your closet to check out all of your "bargains" and find a ton of stuff—but nothing matches, fits, or is appropriate for work;

...you dress for the CEO job instead of the job you want next and everyone wonders how you can afford those clothes on your salary;

...your personal style is so unique that your colleagues notice your shirt coming down the hall before they actually see that it's you; or

...you're a blue jeans person who's stuck in a blue suit workplace.

HUMOR

CHALLENGE: HANDLING STRESS WITH HUMOR

Sam knew how important it was to find ways to keep a healthy perspective at work, so he didn't let the daily stress get to him. He decided to bring in some of his favorite things from home that made him laugh. For example, he pinned Beavis and Butthead comics and photographs of wild fraternity parties on his cubicle walls. Sam also told jokes and stories that he should have reserved for his friends outside of the workplace. When project meetings got tense, Sam typically became very silly and punchy. He often went overboard leading things off track, and alienating others in the process.

SMART MOVES: LAUGHING AWAY TENSION

Whether you favor *The Three Stooges*, *I Love Lucy*, *Seinfeld*, or *Ellen*, most of us turn to sitcoms, movies, cable T.V. comedy specials, or comedy clubs for entertainment. They help us laugh at our common imperfections and keep it all in perspective. To relieve workplace stress that sometimes accompanies tight deadlines and long work-days, it's important to have a good sense of humor. You need to remember not to get so intense about your work that you forget to lighten up sometimes. Unlike Sam, you can give yourself a break while maintaining a professional persona.

Smart Move #69: Keep Small, Silly Items Around

One way to get out of your own way when you're feeling uptight is to look at small, silly items. For example, write a clever, humorous quote on each page of your planner to keep you smiling as you review your "to do" list each day. Or keep a couple of comic strips, wind-up toys, or photographs of you and your friends making silly faces tucked away. Coffee mugs are another convenient place for humorous sayings, comics, or photos. Keeping junk food, such as a jar of gourmet jellybeans, on the corner of your desk is also fun. Just be prepared to attract a lot of visitors who want to grab a bean or two. (And you may find yourself on too much of a sugar high!) Generally, as long as something is in good professional taste, then it's okay to have it around.

Smart Move #70: Tell a Joke

Another way to use humor as a stress-buster is to tell yourself a funny joke when you're getting frustrated. In other words, tell yourself a better story than the one you're dealing with at the time. (Just be careful about sharing your humor with others if it's in questionable taste.)

Smart Move #71: Take a Brief Humor Break

This strategy is equally effective for when you're working under pressure alone or with a group. Consider what's the worst, most ridiculous thing that can happen if your project is late? Come up with a couple of outrageous solutions to sticky problems. Playfully fantasizing about extremes can help you loosen up and generate creative solutions to your dilemma.

Smart Move #72: Go On a Humor Scavenger Hunt

Humor Exercise

Directions: Try to come up with an idea for each category below that you could use at work to help you lighten up. Use your imagination, observations of other people's desks, and conversations with friends to help you generate ideas.

Humorous quotes:

Comic strips:

Small toys:

Photographs:

Coffee Mugs:

Junk/Fun Food:

Funny Jokes:

Humor Breaks:

How To Make Sure You're Laughing All The Way to the Unemployment Line

1) Lead the Macarena during coffee breaks.
2) Incorporate slides of Dilbert comic strips into the quarterly division staff meeting slideshow about the organization's financial performance.
3) Use superglue to affix your colleagues' staplers, calendars, tape dispensers, etc. to the tops of their desks.
4) During a fire drill, sing the jingle for the Slinky commercial while releasing multiple Slinky's down the stairwells.
5) Circulate a false memo among your project team colleagues about a new, tight deadline. Then wait until they panic to tell them the truth.

BURNOUT

CHALLENGE: DEVELOPING STAMINA

Tony worked at his job for eight years. He had mastered the ins and outs long ago and, until recently, hadn't minded doing the same old thing every day. Then he began to feel unsatisfied, wanting more out of his job than the routine tasks. Instead of the usual friendly, energetic Tony, his coworkers greeted a quiet, sullen Tony every morning. After so many years, Tony didn't know what to do to make himself happy again and yet feared making a radical change.

Clarissa felt like she was watching a movie in slow motion. Only it wasn't a movie—it was her life. She had spent the last several months working long hours, worrying constantly about deadlines, and dreaming about what she had to do each day at work. Gradually, she began to feel unmotivated and sluggish. Getting up in the morning to go to work involved hitting the snooze button on her alarm clock at least a half-dozen times. Making it to work on time meant dragging herself halfheartedly through the door at 8:58 a.m. Concentrating on her projects was nearly impossible. Clarissa would cross off another square on her calendar, counting the days until her next vacation. And all she could think of was what she was doing for lunch, after work, and on the weekend. She became increasingly moody and stopped paying attention to her appearance. Others noticed that she was acting erratically and that her hair and clothes were starting to look disheveled.

Alex prided himself on keeping a full schedule, both at work and in his personal life. He frequently worked twelve-hour days, played soccer three nights a week, coached a youth soccer team on Sundays, dated regularly, and took intensive continuing education classes. This schedule worked fine during his first two years out of college. Then he started getting sick at least once a month. He began showing up at work with bags under his eyes, getting only four hours of sleep a night. Alex also began drinking at least two liters of cola a day to remain alert.

COOLING OUT BEFORE IT'S TOO LATE

Burnout is an insidious process. It doesn't happen overnight, but it can still happen intensely and rapidly. There are usually three reasons for burnout. Like Tony, you may be overqualified for a position you've held for a long time. Like Clarissa, you may be overwhelmed by long hours and/or difficult work. Like Alex, you may be overextended, because you're pursuing too many activities at once, on top of a heavy work load. Recovering from burnout takes time, and some radical changes in your lifestyle. The best way to deal with burnout is to prevent it before it starts. If you can identify with any of the scenarios above, or if you're concerned that you may be headed in that direction, you may be burning out or burned out.

Smart Move #73: See If You're Overqualified, Over-whelmed, or Overextended

Burnout has both emotional and physical signs. Although any of these signs may be caused by other things, a pattern of them may also indicate that you're in trouble and need to evaluate your current situation. Use the self-assessment exercise that follows to help you determine if burnout is a reality in your work life.

Burnout Exercise

Directions: Put a "T" next to each statement that is true for you and an "F" next to each one that is false. Count up your total number of "T's" and "F's" and write your totals in the spaces at the bottom of the list. If you have more "T's" than "F's" or if any of your "T's" seems particularly pervasive in your life, then you may be at risk for burnout.

_____ I work 5–7 days a week, and rarely take the time for r&r, exercise, hobbies, or personal relationships.

_____ I often feel unmotivated and hopeless about getting through all of my work.

_____ I depend on large amounts of coffee, diet soda, alcohol, cigarettes, junk food, etc. to keep me going on a regular basis.

_____ I am haunted by the fear of losing my job.

_____ I get run down or sick a lot.

_____ I can't sleep well at night because I'm preoccupied with thoughts of work.

_____ I have frequent mood swings that seem work related.

_____ I feel stuck in a rut at work.

_____ I keep hearing comments from people who know me well that they are worried about me seem stressed out or not like myself lately.

_____ I often feel emotionally numb or empty inside.

Total # of "T's": _____

Total # of "F's": _____

Smart Move #74: Adjust Your Expectations of Yourself and Your Job

Sometimes there's no way to get around projects that require exceptionally long hours or having to work under pressure. During these times, you may lack the time or energy needed to take care of yourself outside of the workplace. You need to do the best you can to meet your personal needs during these times. For example, you need to adjust your expectations so that you can maintain your regular standards in both parts of your life until this little crisis is over. Let your friends, significant others, and family members know up front that you'll be harder to get in touch with during this time. Then do the best you can to keep up-to-date with the most important people in your life. Also, laundry, cooking (if you do it at all), and housekeeping may need to go by the wayside. If someone can help you out, great. If not, get by with the bare minimum for as long as possible. But don't forget to eat, sleep, exercise, play, and take care of your basic needs as much as possible.

Another problem could be that you're bored at work because you're overqualified for your present position. You've either topped out after years of working at the same job, or you're paying dues in a new job. Instead of falling into the burnout abyss, take control of the situation. Adjust your expectations about your job. Recognize that no job can meet all of most people's needs for intellectual and creative stimulation. Seek out new, additional responsibilities, or a change of scenery by relocating. Or look outside of your paid work for challenging activities. Take up a hobby or a sport you've always wanted to pursue, like chess, or sculpting.

Smart Move #75: Get Professional Help

If you feel like you're hitting a brick wall and can't climb over it, walk around it, or blast through it, you may even want to consider getting professional help. Many organizations sponsor an Employee Assistance Program (EAP). This benefit is a free, confidential counseling and referral service. Some employers provide an EAP on-site, while others use off-site services. In either case, the EAP is staffed by independent, professional counselors who are typically social workers and psychologists. They can give you immediate counseling about personal problems—including burnout—and refer you to other professional therapists for short- or long-term help. Such guidance may include stress and time-management techniques. Depending on your insurance coverage, the referred help may be completely or partially covered.

Also consider using a career counselor to help you reevaluate your direction. Professional career counselors can help you assess your skills, interests, values, and personality style, narrow down options, and make an action plan for achieving your goals. They can also provide you with job search coaching and educational advice. Some people seek the guidance of both a therapist and a career counselor to help them recover from burnout. You can use these services simultaneously or consecutively (therapist first then career counselor). Some therapists may focus on career counseling. Make sure that the professional you consult is qualified and has experience with your particular issues. You can contact the American Psychological Association in Washington, D.C. at (202) 336-5500, the National Association of Social Workers in Washington, D.C. at (202) 408-8600, or the American Counseling Association in Alexandria, VA at (703) 823-9800, for information on accredited therapists in your area. You can also contact the National Career Development Association at the same phone number as the American Counseling Association for a referral to a professional career counselor. (For more information on enlisting professionals, see chapter 8 transition resources section.)

Smart Move #76: Turn to Your Support Team

Instead of or in addition to seeking professional help, you can also turn to your support team for advice and emotional sustenance. When you're dealing with burnout, you often feel very alone and disconnected. It's the right time to ask for some extra TLC and guidance from the people in your life who care the most. Your support team is made up of those who you can turn to when you're feeling down as well as when you want to celebrate your victories. Your parents, close friends, mentors (former or current teachers, clergy, more established colleagues, etc.), and any others who you trust and feel safe with are good candidates for your support team. You can ask some members of your team to help you get away from it all; friends and parents may be particularly helpful in this way. Your mentors can help you understand the root of your burnout, your options for dealing with it, and help you to gain valuable perspective on the situation. All members of your support team can potentially help you with both networking resources and reassuring you that you're not a screw-up for feeling burned out. See the chapter 8 transition resources section for more on rallying a support team.

Smart Move #77: Take Time Out

Another option is to take a leave of absence or time out between jobs to get your act together and reconsider your next move. Time out can mean a lot of different things. If you can afford it, you can volunteer, travel, and/or take classes. If you need an income, you can work part-time or at a full-time temporary job that frees up part of your days, evenings, or weekends. Then you can explore your interests and/or rejuvenate during your off-hours. Whatever you decide to do, it's a good idea to try to plan and structure your time out. Otherwise, it's easy to just slip into bumming around, losing your focus, and getting down about the whole thing. Often parents and friends can judge what you're doing as getting off track. This pressure can amplify your own fears and insecurities. So decide what you want to accomplish during your time off and then go for it.

Smart Move #78: Find a Different Job or Career

The real trouble with burnout starts when crisis periods go on without a break. If your career needs don't mesh well with your current job or field, then you may want to consider finding a different job or career path. Everyone is different, so it's a personal judgment call. Also, your values and priorities may change with time. What is okay for you early in your career, for instance, my not be acceptable for you later on.

You have lots of options for exploring other jobs and career paths. These possibilities range from doing your job in another part of your organization, taking a different position within your department or division, or seeking a different position within your organization (see the transferring ins and outs section in chapter 5) to pursuing a position in either a related or unrelated field in another organization. Section III of this book covers the specifics of when and how to change jobs and/or careers.

Bumper Stickers For Beating Burnout

It's important to remember what you really like to do for fun and relaxation. Here is a list of fantasy bumper stickers that may reflect your preference for what you'd rather be doing for a change.

I'd rather be taking a cruise.

I'd rather be dancing all night.

I'd rather be camping.

I'd rather be scuba diving.

I'd rather be reading science fiction techno-thrillers.

I'd rather be shopping.

I'd rather be planting a vegetable garden in my backyard.

I'd rather be sightseeing in Paris.

2

Dealing With Workplace Politics

WORK SMART IQ QUIZ #2

Review each item listed and decide if it's a work smart myth or a work smart reality. In the space before each statement, put an "M" if you think it's a myth and an "R" if you think it's a reality. Then check your responses with the correct answers at the end of the quiz.

_____ **1.** As a newcomer, paying your dues means learning as much as you can about your job and organization as well as proving that you can perform your assigned tasks.

_____ **2.** When you start a new job, you'll earn others' respect by suggesting as many improvements to policies and procedures as you can.

_____ **3.** If you're overwhelmed in your position, keep telling yourself that you should be able to handle it and set ambitious goals for yourself.

_____ **4.** The best way to manage your time during busy work periods is to stop going out socially and to let your hobbies go until your work load lightens up.

_____ **5.** To deal effectively with workplace politics, focus on understanding how things get done and building professional relationships with those people who can help you cut through the red tape.

_____ **6.** In general, the way people actually do behave is a more reliable indicator than what they say is the right way to behave (what to wear, how to conduct work relationships, decorate your desk, spend money, etc.) in your organization.

_____ **7.** Keeping on top of what your manager expects from you on a daily, as well as a long-term, basis is important since his priorities may change frequently.

_____ **8.** Adapt to how your manager prefers updates on your work—by e-mail, memo, in person, or otherwise.

_____ **9.** There are two types of people who you may clash with at work: troublemakers and those who are different from you in terms of personality type, communication style, or agenda.

_____ **10.** Ignoring, confronting, or monitoring a possibly unethical situation are all legitimate responses to it.

Answers: (1)-R, (2)-M, (3)-M, (4)-M, (5)-R, (6)-R, (7)-R, (8)-R, (9)-R, (10)-R

TRANSITIONS

CHALLENGE: SURVIVING THE INITIATION

Mark, an honors graduate from a prestigious liberal arts college, was excited to begin his first job out of college. Riding high from a great senior year, he fully expected to hit the ground running and be a success. For the first six months of his new job, Mark woke up eager to go to work. Then the honeymoon period ended and he began to wonder if he had made a mistake in taking the job. Mark had mastered the technical aspects of his position and was getting bored by the substantial amount of grunt work, and unhappy with his bottom-of-the-ladder status. Worrying that his brain was turning to mush, Mark was crushed to find out that his first performance review was six months away and that it was his organizations' general policy not to promote anyone before eighteen months of service. Since Mark was not feeling challenged, he lost his motivation to make work a priority. Mark resigned himself to feeling frustrated and stuck in a rut.

Elena had the opposite problem. She was in a fast track, entry-level management training position. Rotating through different departments for the first year was stimulating and educational. But it also meant that there was a lot of new information, people, and projects that she needed to keep up with. Elena found that the high volume and intensity of her job was overwhelming at times. She rarely got the chance to sit back and reflect on what was happening. Since the learning curve was steep for her, she spent every free minute trying to get on top of her job. It consumed her personal life on both evenings and weekends. Elena knew that some of her classmates from college would jump at this kind of an opportunity. She started to doubt herself and she secretly yearned for her college lifestyle—days of interesting (but not mind-boggling) classes and nights of socializing with friends.

Rachel's long-term career goal was to become a senior manager. She hated the game of playing politics on the job. She decided to ignore the game and concentrate on getting her work done to the highest standards. Rachel only paid attention to the nuts and bolts of her projects. As a result, she was recognized as a hard worker, but not necessarily star performer material. When senior management conducted their succession planning to identify future senior managers, Rachel was mentioned as a promising candidate for middle management. But everyone agreed that she didn't seem to have what it took to handle the intangible aspects of becoming a top player.

Coping with Newcomer Downs

It's inevitable that, as you make the transition into professional life or into a new organization, you'll have down times. Like Mark, you may feel frustrated by a relative lack of challenge and slow advancement speed. Like Elena, you may feel overwhelmed by a steep learning curve and a lifestyle change. Or like Rachel you may feel consumed by office politics—people's agendas, power struggles, affiliations, and ways of doing things. Stick it out, and your newcomer status will pass. In the meantime, you can try some of the tips we provide below.

Smart Move #79: Jump Out of the Box

If you're facing a relative lack of challenge in your job, find other ways to keep learning and growing. Volunteer to take on extra projects at work. Take in-house or outside classes (see the hot competencies section in chapter 4 and the survival training section in chapter 5). Read more. Become involved in professional associations. Take on, or more actively pursue, a hobby.

Smart Move #80: Play Detective

So the relatively slow advancement speed at your organization is getting you down? Try to reframe this paying dues time as an opportunity for you to really learn all you can about your job and how your organization works. It's the time you're expected to be taking it all in, figuring out how to succeed, and proving yourself. Moreover, by showing that you respect yourself and are highly competent, others will come to respect you as well—and you'll get promoted when the time is right.

Smart Move #81: Prove Your Worth and Respect Your Limits

Suppose you just can't stand your bottom-of-the-ladder status. As long as you don't develop an attitude problem, it will be a temporary situation. You've got to ditch any false sense of entitlement you may have based on your past achievements (see the unnatural disasters section in chapter 5 about a false sense of entitlement when things change). Sure, they've gotten you where you are now. But, whether you're making the transition from being a college senior to a new professional or from one organization to another, it goes with the territory of being a newcomer that you've got to start at the beginning. Once you establish your credibility within your new organization, you'll get promoted.

Also, as a newcomer, it's especially important that you choose your battles. For example, you can't charge into a new organization acting like a know-it-all. As we discussed in the chapter 1 attitude section, you need to be a problem-solver from the start. This means that you need to watch the scope of what you attempt to "solve." One negative extreme is to just raise issues without possible solutions (you'll be labeled a chronic complainer). Another negative extreme is to recommend fixes for established, large-scale practices of the organization up front. Instead, focus on the problem at hand, keeping the big-picture in mind at all times. Eventually—at least six months down the road—you'll have the insight and standing to constructively challenge some of the established practices. So get realistic about what being a newcomer requires. And take the time to appreciate the fresh perspective it offers, rather than focusing on the limits that are inherent in this role.

Smart Move #82: Chunk It Down

You may face a seemingly insurmountable steep learning curve on your new job. Give yourself permission to be a learner by setting realistic goals, breaking what you need to learn into chunks, and you'll soon get the hang of it. And remember, it certainly beats being bored in a job that you're overqualified for.

Smart Move #83: Make Time for Rest and Relaxation

When the lifestyle change that often accompanies a new position makes you reminisce for the good old days, try to maintain the elements of your lifestyle that are most important to you. More flexible hours, for example, may have been a cherished perk of your college years or last job. In your current position, it may be impractical for you to start your weekend on Thursday night. But that doesn't mean you can't go out once or twice with friends during the week and call it a night a little earlier than usual. Before this job, you may have had plenty of time to pursue your favorite hobbies, whereas suddenly you can barely find the time to go grocery shopping or get to the dry cleaner. Even so, it's vital that you at least dabble in one or two interests that are aren't work related. You may not get to rock climb, sing, ride your bicycle, read, or do whatever you love to do that often, but doing some of what you love to do is better than not doing it at all. It will give you a chance to loosen up, have fun, and bring more of your best self to your job.

Smart Move #84: Exploit the System

You have probably realize by now that workplace politics are part of everyone's professional life. Just working hard isn't enough. If you insist on pretending that politics don't exist, or rebel against them, you'll only succeed in sabotaging even your best work efforts. Given that you have a limited amount of energy—what can you do?

Since you can't eliminate workplace politics, the most strategic approach is to change your reaction to it. When people talk about politics, they usually put a negative spin on the topic. For example, they may gripe about how Joe Blow is brown-nosing the powerful department head to get the best projects or how Flo Moe is going to get a promotion before everyone else because she's in tight with her manager. Others get fed up with filling out duplicate requisition forms, getting approval from at least three people, and waiting for over a month to get basic supplies or equipment.

Sometimes, workplace politics may seem to block your path to success. Politics may also require you to follow a procedure to get something accomplished that seems unreasonably tedious. But these situations are out of your control to change. So, focus your energy on getting a grip on what's happening in your workplace. Once you know how to get what you want, you'll build positive working relationships and get your work done. In these ways, becoming politically savvy will enable you to establish credibility within your organization.

Our smart moves throughout the rest of the topics in this chapter—culture, special relationships, and ethics—will teach you some specific ways to become artful and diplomatic within your organization.

Sabotage Your Success As A Newcomer!

1) Complain loudly to the person closest to you about how bored you are.

2) Demand that your manager agree to give you a promotion after six months on the job, since you've clearly paid your dues during your first two quarters.

3) Walk around with a superior attitude, snubbing as many underlings as you can find—temps, college interns, the receptionist, etc.—so that you don't feel as bad about being at the bottom of the professional ladder.

4) When you feel like you're in a new job that's over your head, set large goals for yourself and try to accomplish them all in the shortest time frame possible.

5) As soon as you start your new job, make sure you work most or all of the time, giving up your hobbies and personal life.

6) Bend, break, or blow off the rules when showcasing your achievements on the job.

CULTURE

CHALLENGE: FITTING IN AT YOUR ORGANIZATION

Alex assumed that he had plenty of time to figure out how to fit in at his new job. He didn't want to become employee number 642 and lose his identity as an individual. So Alex didn't listen carefully to the human resources facilitator or any of the other new employees' questions during new employee orientation. He just filled out the necessary paperwork and stared out the window, daydreaming about his weekend plans. When Alex returned to his desk, he put his copy of the policy manual on his bookshelf without even cracking it open. During his first week of work, he got different impressions from different people about how to conduct himself. Depending on who he last spoke with or overheard talking, Alex followed that person's advice. So his behavior was inconsistent and without forethought. When he got confused about how to handle a confusing situation, Alex did whatever he felt like doing at that moment.

BECOMING A CULTURE VULTURE

Your ability to understand an organization's culture (its practices and the underlying beliefs) will help you to succeed as a newcomer. Despite what Alex thought, "fitting in" doesn't have to mean conforming completely to a prototypical mold. Over time, you can choose to what extent you want to express your individuality. Hopefully, you have determined whether or not your organization was good for you before you took the job. But, even if you find you've made a mistake, you can try to make things work out, or change jobs down the road. As a newcomer, the good news is that you can view your workplace with a fresh perspective. The bad news is that it's important for you adapt to your new environment as quickly as possible. This isn't always easy, given that you'll probably get mixed messages about what is the right thing to do in a given situation. So if you don't have much time, and you can't hire a private investigator to solve the mystery for you, what can you do?

Smart Move #85: Pretend You're a Cultural Anthropologist

When a cultural anthropologist investigates a group of people, she uses the participant–observation method. This means that she becomes immersed in the group as an honorary participant and remains detached enough as an observer to really understand how (its practices) and why (the underlying beliefs) the group functions the way it does. As a new employee, you're both an insider and an outsider. In this dual role you can learn from participating directly in your organization's daily rituals, as well as thoughtfully reflecting upon what's normal for your workplace.

Smart Move #86: Listen for Tell Clues

You can look for two kinds of clues about how to succeed: tell clues and show clues. Tell clues are the things that you hear or read. For example, new employee orientations usually include presentations on the history, structure, and current initiatives of the organization, as well as an overview of the basic programs. During such orientations, human resource representatives typically present key information and answer your questions. You may also get a policy manual that documents the organization's policies and procedures concerning things such as work hours, compensation, time off, and resources for seeking psychological, medical, or emergency help, as well as handling grievances. Your manager and peers will also tell you some basics about your job and how to get things done on a daily basis.

Smart Move #87: Look for Show Clues

Show clues, on the other hand, are more subtle than tell clues. Beginning with your interview process, you probably noticed some key things about your workplace. As you spend more time in your new environment, you'll pick up on increasing numbers of show clues. For example, consider the character of your physical surroundings. Do you work in a funky, artistic loft, a glass-fronted high rise, or a renovated Victorian house? Is the furniture designed for comfort, aesthetic effect, or both? Are the desk accessories and equipment old or relatively new? Are they mismatched or uniform? Do many people share resources such as computer printers? Are there recycling bins for items like paper, cans, and bottles? Do employees display personal momentos, such as family photographs, quotes, toys, and plants in their spaces? If so, what kinds of items seem most prevalent? Which ones, if any, seem to be conspicuously missing and therefore probably taboo?

Another important show clue concerns the layout of work spaces. Are the floors populated mainly by cubes or just open spaces with no dividers? Do people have permanent desk assignments or do they sign up for work areas for when they are in the office? Are there many employees sitting closely together or is there a lot of space between people's desks? Are similar departments grouped together or are they scattered throughout a floor or building?

How receptionists, your boss, and others answer the telephone, further reveals unwritten codes of conduct. Are employee responses formal or informal? Is there a standard phone response line or does it vary widely? If you're on hold, does the local soft rock radio station, classical music, the organization's advertising jingle, or no music at all play?

Working styles also clue you in to the cultural dynamics. Do people seem to work more independently in their own spaces or cluster together in small work groups? Are there often many meetings going on? When and where do meetings occur most frequently—in conference rooms, in someone's office, over lunch, or at other times and places?

Smart Move #88: Clarify Mixed Messages

While gathering show and tell clues, you may get confused by mixed messages. For example, in some organizations, employees may show up everyday wearing jeans or casual work clothes. They may be especially friendly with each other, hanging out at lunch or after work to share stories or jokes. They may even sit closely together in fairly open work spaces that don't automatically designate who's on top, like a corner office would.

However, despite these clues that the organization is pretty low key about their clothes, relationships, and work spaces, you may also notice that there are still certain implicit rules that seem more rigid. For example, people rarely take a real lunch break. Instead, they work alone while they eat or have meetings over lunch. And everybody arrives by 8:00 a.m. and leaves no earlier than 6:30 p.m., even though the official work hours are 9:00 a.m. to 5:30 p.m.

How do you reconcile such mixed messages? In general, show clues are usually more reliable than tell clues. That is, unless your manager is the one telling you how to behave. Then go with what your manager advises you to do. Also, you want to model your behavior after your most successful, ethical colleagues, rather than after those irreverent, lucky ones. Believe it or not, if you rail against the cultural rules too long, the karma boomerang will get you sooner or later.

It's also important to ask for clarification if you're unclear about something. One example of a confusing issue that's common when times are financially tight, concerns how you spend money on the job. In some organizations, watching every penny doesn't just apply to the big stuff. It means watching the bottom line about office supplies (yes, like binder clips and pens). Even if you're doing a great job about the big stuff, you still need to go with the flow on the little things. Otherwise, your seemingly little oversights will eclipse your larger efforts (see the bottom line section in chapter 4).

Some policy manuals are not updated regularly. Instead you may receive a memo or attend a large, organization- or division-wide meeting about the organization's approach or philosophy. You may get plaques, paperweights, mugs, or other paraphernalia that advertise the company's mission, statement, or values—only to discover that the middle managers in the organization are not necessarily walking the talk. That is, they're still doing things in a way that doesn't jive with what you understand to be the status quo. Realize that sometimes it takes time for a new approach to trickle down, and that sometimes there's a lot of internal conflict among management about priorities and business styles, especially after a restructuring or merger.

Smart Move #89: Evaluate Your Organization's Culture

Culture Exercise

Directions: List the top three tell clues about your organization's culture that others have formally conveyed to you. Then list the top three show clues that you've picked up through just being in your workplace. Next, list any rules of the game that seem confusing based on your tell and show clues information. Finally, indicate how you can reconcile each mixed message.

Tell Clues (intentionally presented to you by others)

From new employee orientation:

1.

2.

3.

From employee policy manual:

1.

2.

3.

From your manager and peers:

1.

2.

3.

From another source _____:

1.

2.

3.

Show Clues (casually observed by you)

About your physical surroundings (style of office, furniture, shared resources, recycling bins, personal momentos on desks, etc.):

1.

2.

3

Layout of work spaces (cubes or open spaces, permanent or temporary desk assignments, space or cramped between desks, departments grouped together, or scattered, etc.):

1.

2.

3.

Other (how others answer the telephone, ratio independent versus group work, frequency of meetings, and locations of meetings, etc.):

1.

2.

3.

Mixed Messages (discrepancies between tell and show clues)

1.

2.

3.

Reconciliation of Mixed Messages

1.

2.

3.

Smart Move #90: Know When to Stop Analyzing and When to Start Again

Unlike a real anthropologist, your goal isn't to understand and document, and then return to your native society. As a new employee, your ultimate objective is to adapt to your organization's culture well enough to become a fully accepted member of that organization for the duration of your employment. You want to be an insider. Of course, you always want to be able to analyze and deal with changes in the organization's cultural rules. You can always use your accomplishment log (see the accomplishment logs section in chapter 3) or your mentor (see the mentors section in chapter 3). You can also help yourself by taking time to reflect on the latest changes in your company during your time off. (In addition, chapter 5 will help you to manage your career during times of organizational change.)

Five Signs That You're Culturally Clueless

1) You use your copy of the employee policy manual for scrap paper.

2) You put in a requisition for your own computer printer even though everyone around you shares printers.

3) You record a general, casual voice mail message for your phone line that you leave on all the time. But everybody else's voice mail messages vary by what they're up to each day and include a back-up referral if they're out.

4) You consistently bolt for the door at 5:30 p.m. sharp, the official end of the workday, while the rest of your department stays until at least 7:00 p.m. every night.

5) You reconcile mixed messages about the right thing to do by tossing a coin or following the lead of the office rebel.

EXPECTATIONS

CHALLENGE: KNOWING WHAT'S REALISTIC

Tim read his job description when he came on board at his new organization. And he understood all of his new projects as they came up every few months. Tim randomly addressed his responsibilities, depending upon what appealed most to him at the time. He often wondered, however, why he seemed to never get on top of his work. Every time Tim felt like he was making progress on one project, his manager suddenly seemed to need another one finished right away. Sometimes Tim felt frustrated, but he chalked it up to the nature of his fast-paced, high-volume organization.

Whenever Nicole had a question, she sent her manager an e-mail. Her manager responded by leaving her a voice mail or stopping by her desk to talk with her about it. The manager never returned Nicole's e-mails, but Nicole rarely initiated speaking with her manager in person. Nicole's manager frequently encouraged her department members to communicate their concerns as they arose. But Nicole couldn't understand why her manager seemed unreceptive to her particular questions.

Cameron often disguised his criticisms as questions. He frequently asked/told his manager that something should be done differently: "Shouldn't the layout of the department staff's desks be arranged this way? Shouldn't our e-mail addresses be linked that way? Shouldn't there be two weeks extra lead time on projects?" Since Cameron challenged so many aspects of the way his manager and his organization did things, his manager didn't take him seriously. He perceived Cameron as an egotistical know-it-all.

Tara's primary concern was making sure that her manager knew what a great job she was doing every day. She wasn't overly concerned with what her peers thought of her and went through the motions when it came to team projects. Tara didn't go out of her way to communicate with her teammates about new developments or show them any appreciation for their work. They knew that she wasn't really a team player, and they didn't enjoy working with her. Ultimately, Tara's coworkers stopped keeping her in the loop and showed her up for who she really was—a self-interested brown-noser.

IDENTIFYING AND DEALING WITH OTHERS' DEMANDS

You probably know pretty much how you like to work and what you want out of your career as you progress. But knowing this isn't enough. You may need to manage others' expectations of you as well, in order to succeed. It can be messy both understanding what your manager's, peer's, and own expectations are—and then juggling them from day to day. But if you don't at least give it a try, you'll end up sabotaging your career like Tim, Nicole, Cameron, and Tara.

Smart Move #91: Keep on Top of Your Manager's Short- and Long-Term Expectations

You need to understand the requirements of your job on a big-picture level. You may or may not have a written job description. You may even participate in creating your own job description with your manager. Whichever the case, make sure that you know what's up from the beginning. You also need to keep on top of what your manager expects of you on a daily, as well as long-term basis. It's important that you know which of your responsibilities your manager prioritizes over others. These priorities may change frequently, depending on business needs.

Smart Move #92: Communicate With Your Manager in Their Preferred Style

You and your manager need to find ways of communicating on a regular basis about the status of your projects and hot issues. Some managers have more of a hands-on style of managing, while others are rarely around. The extremes of these styles may cause you problems. For instance, if you have a manager who's checking in with you once an hour to see how things are going and asking you a million questions about every little thing, you may feel like a little kid who can't do anything by yourself. On the other hand, if your manager is never around, doesn't return your messages, and leaves you feeling directionless or constantly overloaded, you've got big problems.

A more balanced approach would be for you and your manager to have periodic performance reviews, one-on-one meetings, and department staff meetings. You also need to understand how your manager prefers for you to communicate with him—by e-mail, memo, in person, or otherwise. It's important that you check out what your manager's communication preferences are and then try to adapt to them. This will keep your relationship running smoothly.

Smart Move #93: Choose Your Battles

It's inevitable that at some point your manager may tell you to do something that you believe is unreasonable. When this happens, you must make a choice. You can just follow your instructions, or you can talk it over with your manager and let her know how you feel. For example, she may ask you to complete an assignment within a time frame that's not humanly possible. You can let her know that you want to do a good job but need some help to complete the project. You might want to suggest that the deadline be moved. A good manager will be responsive to an employee who constructively lets her know when something doesn't seem right.

Whatever you do, remember to choose your battles. You don't want to complain every time your manager gives you a directive, or you'll develop a reputation either as a whiner or as someone who shies away from a challenge. Conversely, you don't want to always do what you're told no matter what, or you'll be perceived as a doormat, or worse, as someone who doesn't keep their manager from being blindsided by a bad situation.

Smart Move #94: Consider Your Coworkers' Expectations

As if your own and your manager's expectations weren't enough to juggle, you also have to consider your coworkers' expectations. Your peers and subordinates (if you have any) expect you to be attentive to their needs and challenges. Naturally, they need you to keep them in the information loop about any relevant happenings that affect their work. And you must treat your coworkers with respect at all times. That means doing things like listening carefully to what they say; speaking and writing to them in courteous tones; letting them know that you value their time and hard work; helping them when they're in a bind; and being a team player when you work together on projects.

Sometimes you'll hear about how well you meet your coworkers' expectations directly from them—for better or for worse. You'll also get feedback through the performance review process, and your manager may get what's called 360-degree feedback about you. Your manager may survey on paper and/or in person several other people at different levels who you come into contact with regularly, to determine how you come across to others on the job.

Smart Move #95: Know the Assumptions and Implications of Managing Expectations

There are three key underlying assumptions and implications of managing others' expectations. One assumption is that these expectations are partially objective and partially subjective. Generally, everyone will expect you to meet your job requirements and follow common business protocol. But the relative importance of each of these things, as well as other expectations, may vary from person to person. The main implication of this assumption is that you need to proactively seek to identify and understand others' expectations of you in order to succeed.

Another assumption you need to make is that some colleagues may not expect from you the same things as others. Try to sort through and manage these expectations as best you can—without becoming a chameleon. Prioritize whose expectations are most important to you and your success.

A third assumption is that these expectations may or may not reflect reality. The implication of this assumption is that you need to weigh and carefully decide how to react to expectations on a case by case basis. This is especially true if your manager or coworker expects you to do something that you think may be unethical (see the ethics section in chapter 2).

Smart Move #96: Identify Others' Expectations, Define Your Difficult Situation and Reactions, and Evaluate the Outcomes

Expectations Exercise

Directions: The first section of the worksheet is for you to clarify your manager's and coworkers' overall expectations of you. The second section is for you to consider both the specific expectations that are difficult for you to handle, along with how you've managed these kinds of situations in the past. The third section is for you to evaluate how well your strategies for managing difficult expectations have worked and what, if anything, you'd do differently in the future.

I. Identify Others' Expectations

   A. Your Manager's General Expectations:

   Job Requirements:

   Current Short-Term Priorities:

   Current Long-Term Priorities:

   Regular Reality Checks

   (performance reviews, one on one meetings, dept. staff meetings, etc.):

   Manager's Preferred Communication Style

   (hands-on, hands-off, by phone, e-mail, in -person, etc.):

   B. Your Coworkers Generally Expect You to (check all that apply):

   _____ Listen actively to their concerns and points of view.

   _____ Write to them clearly, concisely, and courteously.

   _____ Show appreciation for their efforts.

   _____ Demonstrate willingness to help them in a bind.

   _____ Be a team player on projects.

   _____ Other: _____

II. Define Your Difficult Situations and Reactions

   A. Your Difficult Situations

   When have other's expectations caused you problems? Check all that apply:

   _____ My manager has directed me to meet a deadline that I perceived as unrealistic.

_____ My manager or coworker has insisted that I take an approach to a project that I strongly disagreed with, or thought that I had a better way of doing.

_____ My manager has given me performance review feedback from himself or others that I believed was off the mark.

_____ My manager and coworkers have communicated mutually exclusive expectations or priorities to me, creating a no win situation.

_____ My manager's style is so hands-off that I must function with minimal supervision, even under circumstances that require her input.

_____ My manager is so hands-on that I feel like someone is always hovering over my shoulder, monitoring my every move.

_____ My manager's or coworker's preferred style of communicating is totally different than my preferred style of communicating.

_____ Other:

B. Your Reactions

What strategies have you used to manage others' expectations of you in difficult situations like the above ones? Check all that apply:

_____ I challenged my manager or coworkers about their ex-pectations.

_____ I let something go that I disagreed with, but I don't do this all the time.

_____ I tried to please everyone.

_____ I discussed the expectations of the project with my manager or coworkers.

_____ I prioritized my expectations over others' expectations.

_____ I tried to meet my manager's or coworker's expectations by adapting to their way of thinking.

_____ Other:

III. Evaluate the Outcomes

What was the result of each of your choices for managing others' expectations of you? How could you approach these situations differently, if need be, in the future? Copy each expectation and your reaction, or strategy, from Part II in the spaces that follow.

Then fill in the outcome of each choice along with what you'd do differently next time.

Expectation #1:
Your Reaction (Strategy):
The Outcome:
New or Modified Smart Move:
Expectation #2:
Your Reaction (Strategy):
The Outcome:
New or Modified Smart Move:
Expectation #3:
Your Reaction (Strategy):
The Outcome:
New or Modified Smart Move:
Expectation #4:
Your Reaction (Strategy):
The Outcome:
New or Modified Smart Move:
Expectation #5:
Your Reaction (Strategy):
The Outcome:
New or Modified Smart Move:
Expectation #6:
Your Reaction (Strategy):
The Outcome:
New or Modified Smart Move:
Expectation #7:
Your Reaction (Strategy):
The Outcome:
New or Modified Smart Move:

Guidelines For Mismanaging Expectations

1) Prioritize your daily responsibilities based on what you feel like doing at the moment.

2) Write your manager voluminous e-mails with project updates and questions, despite the fact that the has repeatedly told you that he prefer concise, verbal communications at the end of each day.

3) Every time your manager asks you to do something that you think is unreasonable, become defensive.

4) Ignore your coworkers' demands and feedback—since the only one whose opinion really matters is your manager's.

5) Try to please everyone all of the time.

6) Never reevaluate how well your strategies for managing others' expectations are working. Instead, approach every day as if yesterday never happened.

SPECIAL RELATIONSHIPS

CHALLENGE: DEALING WITH FRIENDS, SIGNIFICANT OTHERS, RELATIVES, MULTIPLE BOSSES, AND CLASHERS

Peter had been friends with Chris since they both first started at their organization two years ago. Then Peter got promoted to a level above Chris and ended up supervising him on a project team for six months. Suddenly, their easygoing relationship wasn't so easygoing. Peter sensed that there was unspoken tension between the two of them, and wasn't sure what to do. Hoping that it was just his imagination, Peter buried himself in the project. He continued to be extra friendly to Chris on the job and at a local bar that was a popular office hangout. Peter confided in Chris about issues related to the project that were difficult for him, including problems with other team members. Chris was receptive to hearing the inside scoop on Peter's work life.

But the other team members and Peter's manager felt that Chris and Peter's friendship was inappropriate. Peter's project team members resented that he was playing favorites, and didn't trust him to be objective about their contributions. They also felt uneasy going to him with problems that they wanted to remain confidential. Peter's manager told him that he had to learn to handle the added responsibility of setting limits that came with his promotion. Peter worried that he'd screwed up his first big project in his new role and abruptly changed his behavior with Chris. Peter announced to Chris that he couldn't share certain things with him anymore and had to keep his distance at work and during after work gatherings. Chris didn't take the news well. He told Peter that his promotion had obviously gone to his head and that he didn't want to be friends with someone on a power trip anyway.

Marissa hadn't been in a serious relationship in a couple of years. After working every day for several months with one of her division managers, Joe, he asked her out to lunch. They had a great time and their work relationship evolved into a serious, personal one. For a couple of months, Marissa and Joe were happily caught up in the rush of a new romance. Whenever Marissa's coworkers asked her if she was dating anyone, she avoided answering the question directly or responded, "Not seriously." At first, this didn't bother her, since she felt like it was her exciting little secret. But as time passed, sneaking around took its toll on her. She didn't like lying to her colleagues and felt left out of their lunchtime discussions about their significant others. It also became awkward to resist a couple of her closer work friends' invitations to fix her up. Marissa also couldn't accompany Joe to holiday parties and other work-related events. Each time, she got increasingly upset. And she also had trouble keeping her emotions under wraps at work when she and Joe had problems in their personal relationship.

After establishing herself in her career field for a few years, Fiora went to work for her father in the family business. Since she'd already gained experience elsewhere, they both thought it would be an easy transition. From the first day, however, it became a difficult situation. Fiora and her father both tried to manipulate each other into doing things their way, rather than talking it out professionally. Also, anytime Fiora had a family problem, she brought it up during work hours. Fiora and her father often ended up arguing heatedly. After one particularly nasty argument, Fiora confided in her coworker, Vicki. Vicki then repeated the story to another coworker, who spread it around the organization. By the next day, the story had circulated back to Fiora's father. He was furious with Fiora for sharing their personal business in his organization and their personal and professional relationships became more distant.

Jordan was hired to work as the assistant to two comanagers of his department. He figured it would be a good opportunity to work with two very different people. They had each seemed easygoing and willing to train him when he interviewed with them separately. After a couple of weeks on the job, however, Jordan discovered that he'd stepped into a nightmare situation. Jordan's managers were so busy that they didn't communicate with him about his work load very often. When Jordan tried to let either of them know that he had too much work, they'd just tell him to figure it out. Or they'd just reiterate that their work was important and had to get done first. After a couple of months of trying to keep up with a double work load, Jordan felt so frustrated and incompetent that he quit.

Tom met Suzanne his first day. She befriended him quickly—inviting him to join her for lunch, offering to show him the ropes, and schmoozing with him about office politics. At first Tom thought Suzanne was just a really outgoing colleague. Then he discovered that she ingratiated herself to everyone so that she could find out their fears and manipulate them to her own advantage. She was a gossip, too, who often dropped innuendoes in staff meetings and other public places, making people embarrassed and angry at her.

Tom's colleagues had different ways of handling Suzanne. Some ignored her bad behavior. Others called her on it directly, telling her to cut it out. Tom, however, was so unnerved at the thought of becoming her next victim that he became preoccupied with preventing this from happening. He vigilantly monitored whether Suzanne was in earshot and what he said in front of her. Tom also tried to be super nice to her, hoping that she'd choose someone else as her next target. Suzanne realized that Tom was intimidated by her, and this fed her false sense of power. Eventually, Tom became so distracted by Suzanne's antics that his performance suffered.

ESTABLISHING BOUNDARIES

Developing appropriate relationships with your colleagues is a vital part of your work life. How do you set boundaries with work friendships so that you don't have Peter's problem with Chris? Is it okay to date colleagues, or are you doomed to end up like Marissa and Joe? Is it possible to work well with relatives, or will you go nuts like Fiora and her father? How can you work for multiple bosses without getting pulled in several directions at once like Jordan? And how do you handle clashing colleagues like Suzanne, without becoming live bait like Tom did?

Smart Move #97: Set Limits with Friends at Work

There's nothing intrinsically wrong with making friends at work. The problems come in when the friendships possibly interfere with your professional relationships. For example, you may become buddies with a peer who you then have to supervise on either a project or in a full-time capacity. When the balance of power shifts in your favor, both you and your friend may end up feeling uncomfortable.

If this happens, you need to be up front with your friend about the situation. You don't have to stop being friends, but you do need to separate your roles as friends and professionals. For both of your sakes, it's important that you don't play favorites or give anyone that impression. Others, knowing that you're friends, may be concerned about this possibility.

Monitor what you discuss with your friend about work when you become his temporary or full-time manager. In the past, you may have freely talked about issues or people that were bothering you, over dinner or a drink. You no longer have this luxury and need to set more clearly defined boundaries about what's off-limits. Hopefully, your friend will respect your needs and understand that redefining your relationship will be mutually beneficial. If not, then you'll have to decide what's more important to you—your career or retaining your friend (who's not supportive of your needs).

Smart Move #98: Evaluate the Risks of Dating and Be Discreet

Finding the right balance in work friendships is easy as compared with dealing with dating colleagues. A lot of it depends on your relative positions in the organization. Obviously, dating someone who works closely with you is riskier than dating someone who's in a different division or location. And dating someone who is your peer is preferable to dating someone who is either above or below you in status. Regardless of these things, however, you still risk difficulties in your personal relationship. Worse, a break-up will certainly strain your professional relationship.

Discretion is very important. It may be tough to keep your private life to yourself when you have to be on guard about it at work and at work-related events where people may bring significant others. Generally, it's better to keep your work and personal lives completely separate. If you and a close colleague really want to develop a meaningful personal relationship, it's in your mutual best interests to consider having one of you move to a different area of the organization or even to a different organization.

Smart Move #99: Separate Work and Home Relationships with Family Members

There are several different scenarios whereby you may work with a relative. For example, you could work in a family business or at an organization where a relative also works. In either of these settings, you may work with a parent, grandparent, uncle, aunt, or cousin. Whatever the case is, the best way to work smart is to differentiate between your work and home relationships as much as possible.

One way to do this is to not take advantage of your personal connection with the other person. In order to maintain a sense of professionalism, you can't intentionally push to get your way. And you can't manipulate them into doing what you want all of the time. Otherwise you'll end up aggravated about getting manipulated back on a personal level most of the time. Essentially, you can't have it both ways—personal and professional—at the same time.

Sometimes it's helpful to create mutually agreed upon rules for how to separate your work and personal relationships. For example, you may decide that you won't discuss your personal problems at work (especially controversial issues related to your family).

Another approach is to remain as objective as possible about your professional disagreements. Becoming highly emotional is never helpful in a work setting. And it can become particularly explosive when it's with a relative.

When you're working with a relative, you also need to be extra careful about who you confide in. Do not share personal or professional information that may be hurtful, or damage the credibility of your relative, with anyone. Doing so only opens yourself up to trouble if you become estranged from someone you've confided in. Even if someone slips up and circulates gossip around the office without being malicious, you're in trouble. It'll be hard to earn your relative's trust again. And, in the meantime, you'll also have to deal with repercussions from your family about the situation. When in doubt, don't talk about anything that may come back to haunt you or cause rifts in your personal life.

It's important to make sure that you have ample time apart from your relative. Some spouses, siblings, and even parents and children work really well together 99 percent of the time. But without a break, it's inevitable that you'll start getting on each other's nerves. This is especially important if you work and live with your relative. Make sure to take some personal or vacation days separately or have outside interests that you pursue on your own.

Smart Move #100: Connect the Dots Between Managers

There are various situations that involve reporting to more than one manager. For example, you may participate in a training program that involves rotating through several different departments during the course of a year. In this case, you may report simultaneously to a training program manager and a department manager during each phase of your rotation. While your department manager will give you specific projects to work on, you may also need to keep in touch with your training program manager. There may be formal program meetings for all of the participants or mini performance reviews that involve your training program manager. Or you may not even have a training program manager. Either way, you need to concentrate on adjusting to different department managers' styles in very short periods of time. This can be tough, because you're focusing on new tasks and new people all at once. And, just as you get the hang of both, you'll rotate into a new situation. The upside to this scenario is that you get exposed to many different areas and people in your organization, which will allow you to determine the best fit for your career interests and personality style.

Another multiple manager situation is one in which you permanently report to two managers. Sometimes a department manager saves money in their budget by having two managers share a direct report. If both managers have equal levels of authority and are under pressure, each one may demand that you focus on their work over the other's. This can be difficult for you, especially if the two managers don't communicate with each other. Worse, they may not communicate with each other because they don't get along. If this is the case, you'll be caught in the middle, constantly trying to figure out how to get two full work loads done and keep the peace.

You may want to suggest that the three of you have a meeting to discuss how to divide up your work effectively on an ongoing basis. For instance, you may be assigned to one manager for three days a week and the other for the remaining two days. But it can be tough when both managers still expect you to complete your work by deadlines that fall on your "off" days. Whatever you do, don't tolerate being in the middle for long. You'll only run yourself ragged trying to handle a superhuman work load, and they'll take advantage of you more and more as time goes on. If they up the ante too much, you'll eventually fail and have to take the blame for it.

Some people, however, enjoy working for two managers, especially if there's a real sense of teamwork among all of you. So don't assume the worst until you check out the specific circumstances and the people involved.

You may work officially for one manager and have an unofficial, dotted-line relationship with another. A dotted-line relationship is one in which you do work for a second manager on an as-needed basis. This situation is harder in some ways than having two official managers. It's also easier in some ways. On the downside, your dotted-line manager may expect you to be available at a moment's notice. This is especially true if she is more senior than your primary manager. Certainly, your primary manager should defer in this case. But if she doesn't, you're stuck in a situation similar to the dual manager scenario we just described.

You may dislike working for your secondary manager. In this case it's easier to have a dotted-line relationship, because your secondary manager is generally less demanding. Also, you gain the benefit of doing diverse work and developing a professional relationship with someone who could help you advance in your career. Again, the most important thing when working in any multiple manager situation is to communicate with both managers about the full scope of your responsibilities and to clarify their priorities consistently.

Smart Move #101: Know Your Type of Clasher

During every phase of your career, you'll deal with clashers—people who rub you the wrong way and who you dread dealing with. There are two types of clashers: Troublemakers and those who are simply different from you in some way. Troublemakers intentionally and maliciously try to get ahead at others' expense and like to stir things up. A troublemaker may spread rumors about people to try to ruin others' reputations. Or a troublemaker may be seemingly friendly, but talk negatively about you behind your back. Regardless of the tactics, you may wonder if it's possible to handle these kinds of colleagues without going crazy or spending every minute of your day dealing with it. The best way to address a troublemaker is to avoid her as much as possible. When you can't steer clear of her, don't stoop to her level or react to her prompts. It will only escalate her behavior and end up reflecting poorly on you. Instead, try to keep your interactions with her straightforward and brief.

Other people clash with you simply because they have a different personality type, communication style, or agenda than you. For example, just because someone is more outgoing or is more withdrawn; prefers to share information verbally or favors writing; or values creativity or prizes stability doesn't mean that he's out to get you. It just means that you need to work a little harder to respect him and bridge the difference gaps. You have to understand people on their terms to get along. And you have to in order to get along to get ahead.

ETHICS

CHALLENGE: DEMONSTRATING INTEGRITY

Garrett's friend Susan from another department asked him how much he earned. Garrett replied, "Enough." Susan persisted, and Garrett replied that he'd rather not discuss it. Susan continued to press, saying that it wasn't a big deal since she'd shared her salary with him. Garrett became uncomfortable and bowed to the pressure. He mumbled that he earned around x dollars and changed the subject. Much to his surprise, one of his other friends got fired later that week when his manager learned that he was discussing his compensation with his coworkers.

Oscar sat behind his colleague, Melissa, in a cubicle. They worked together frequently on special projects and reported to the same manager. He knew that she had been having trouble lately with her boyfriend, because he overheard part of an argument on the phone. At the end of the day, Oscar and Melissa happened to leave work at the same time. As they walked to the elevator together, Oscar commented to Melissa that it sounded like she had a heavy-duty fight with her boyfriend that afternoon. Stunned, Melissa blushed, said that she forgot something at her desk, and encouraged Oscar to go ahead without her. She turned quickly away and rushed back toward the direction of her cube. From that point on, Melissa distanced herself from Oscar, and their work relationship became strained.

Nancy's colleagues swung by her desk to pick her up for a birthday lunch. She'd been buried for the last several hours in paperwork related to the performance review process, which was spread all over her desktop. A draft of her feedback about her colleagues was clearly visible on her computer screen. Nancy had lost track of the time and didn't want to keep the others waiting, so she grabbed her coat and headed out the door. While Nancy was at lunch, several people came looking for her and left notes on her desk. Her manager was one of these people. When she saw that Nancy had left confidential information both on her desk and computer screen, she wrote her a note requesting that she see her at once.

Paula found it overwhelming to balance her busy schedule at work with personal business. Whenever she got a free moment in between meetings or project deadlines, she made a phone call from her desk. She regularly called her health insurance company to inquire about the status of her benefits, her credit card company to discuss billing issues, and her doctors to schedule appointments or discuss problems. Since Paula made her calls at random times, there were often lots of other people around. She tried to keep her personal phone conversations brief and figured that no one really noticed since they were scattered throughout the day. But others often overheard her on the phone talking about something that was clearly personal, and it seemed to many of them that it happened a lot.

Preventing and Reacting to Unethical Situations

There are a range of unethical and potentially unethical situations in every workplace. If you act unethically, you may face disciplinary action, end up on probation, or even get fired. Most clear-cut, unethical situations fall into one of three categories: things you shouldn't say; things you shouldn't leave out; and things you shouldn't take. You can learn how to prevent acting unethically in blatant situations like the ones that Garrett, Oscar, Nancy, and Paula faced by following the guidelines in Smart Moves 102-113. You can learn how to react to questionable situations by following the guidelines in Smart Move 114.

Smart Move #102: Keep Secrets to Yourself

As Garrett found out, sometimes nosy people will press you to reveal private information about yourself or others. The first category, things you shouldn't say, includes the fact that you shouldn't gossip or reveal information like compensation levels. Simply tell anyone who asks that you don't want to discuss such information. It's your responsibility to help maintain a professional, ethical work environment by respecting everyone's privacy.

Similarly, you may accidentally overhear your colleague's private phone conversations. As Oscar discovered, the best thing to do if you overhear someone's personal business is to pretend that you didn't hear anything. Unless that person asks you directly if you overheard his conversation, don't casually mention it to him. These situations can become uncomfortable, especially when you sit near a coworker who, like Melissa, frequently gets into arguments or steamy asides with her mate.

Smart Move #103: Keep Private Documents Private

It's easy to walk away from your desk for a minute—to go to the bathroom, a meeting, or lunch—without noticing what's on it. And sometimes you may be in the midst of working on projects that involve sensitive or confidential information. That's why, as Nancy experienced, you have to be careful not to accidentally leave out documents that are private. It's vital that you always put away—and preferably lock away—any hard copy that others shouldn't stumble across. Such papers may include yours or others' compensation, performance reviews, personal contact information, medical status, or other documents that are for your eyes only. Standing files on your desktop or sideboard are not necessarily a deterrent for curious bypassers, whether they're from inside or outside of your organization. Remember, too, that this kind of information can be on your computer screen as well. So secure it by shutting down or password protecting your computer as well as clearing off your desk before you walk away. And do these things every time you leave your desk, not just at the end of your workday.

Smart Move #104: Use Work Supplies for Work

Many people don't believe that taking home a box of paper clips, a stapler, or even a ream of printer paper is really stealing from their organization. It is. Although you may not get paid very much, you're not entitled to help yourself to the supply cabinet whenever you feel like it. The exception is if you need supplies to work on a project at home. Then only take what you need to complete the work. And don't stock up, just in case another project may require supplies. Take it one project at a time. It's like littering— it may not be that big of a deal if only one person does it, but when everyone does it, the results are disastrous.

Smart Move #105: Accept Gifts at Your Own Risk

In addition to supplies, gifts from outside clients may be off-limits. Check out your organization's formal or informal policy about accepting them. For example, some clients (especially during the winter holidays) will send expensive gifts to persuade you to throw more business their way. Some organizations say that it's okay for you to take all gifts. Some organizations allow you to keep gifts that are under a certain dollar value. Some organizations let you know that it's an unacceptable practice, because you may give the sender the message that you'll favor them in some way. This, of course, is unethical.

Smart Move #106: Make Personal Calls Brief

There are also many intangible things you shouldn't take. One of these things is your organization's time. For example, it's inevitable that you'll need to make an occasional personal call during work hours. If you make more than occasional phone calls, especially long distance ones, you're actually stealing time and money from your employer. Also, as Paula found out, your colleagues may overhear your discussions with your doctor's office, significant other, family members, or credit card company. So it's a good idea to try to make these calls early in the morning, during lunch, or late in the day when there are fewer people around. And reserve truly personal conversations for before or after work.

Smart Move #107: Surf the Net for Pleasure at Home

Another time buster at work is the Internet. Many offices now have Internet connections for work-related research and communication. It may be tempting to spend some time writing e-mails to your friends, looking at sites related to your hobbies, or just wandering around. Time can pass really quickly when you're on the Net, whether it's for work or pleasure. So stick to the business at hand when you're at work. Play with the Net on your own time.

Smart Move #108: Make Time—Not Excuses—at Work

Another way to take your organization's time relates to your work hours. For example, some people chronically come in late, take long lunches, and leave early whenever possible. You may get away with occasionally shaving time off of your workday. If you do it all of the time, though, your manager will notice what's up and you'll get in trouble. This is true even if you try to cover your tracks with "good" excuses related to work. Explanations like, "I was consulting with a colleague on another floor"; "I was picking up something for a project at a local store"; or "I was in a meeting across town that ran late," only work once in a while. If your manager needs to find you and you're not where you're supposed to be, the reason won't matter.

Smart Move #109: Use Days Off When You Really Need Them

A related no-no concerns abusing sick and personal days. Everyone needs time off to recharge once in a while. Vacation days are intended for rest and relaxation. Personal days, if you have them, are meant for you to take care of personal business that you normally need to do during work hours, such as getting a driver's license. Sick days are there for when you're really feeling under the weather. The problem occurs when you take an excessive number of them during the course of a year. In case you get genuinely ill, depending on what state you live in and how large your organization is, there are state and federal provisions for taking consecutive time off. Check with your organization's human resources department for more information. But if you're just trying to take off time to play while getting paid, watch out. You'll get nailed sooner or later.

Smart Move #110: Give Your Colleagues Lead Time

A second intangible set of things you shouldn't take concerns taking advantage of your coworkers. For example, don't take advantage of others' time, especially if you're in a position of power over them. Try to give others as much notice as possible when you need something, rather than approaching them at the last minute (for the third time that week).

Smart Move #111: Grab the Glory with Your Own Ideas and Products

Don't take credit for others' ideas or finished products. As we'll discuss in chapter 3's credit section, giving credit will help you shine. It will make you look (as well as feel) good to acknowledge others' achievements. Besides which, taking others' glory is highly unethical. And you'll antagonize the people who deserve the credit as well as your manager.

Smart Move #112: Check Out Who Owns It Before You Sell It

A third intangible set of things you shouldn't take concerns your organization's intellectual property. Carefully read your employment contract when you accept your position. Inventing or improving a product or service yourself on the job doesn't necessarily mean you own it. Usually, the organization owns the rights to it. So don't go running off to patent something before you make sure it's really yours, free and clear.

Smart Move #113: Show Stuff to Outsiders Selectively

When you're interviewing with another organization or leave an organization, be careful about what samples of your work you show to outsiders. Again, your work probably legally belongs to the employer, not to you. If you need to prove that you can do what you say (develop programs, write policies, document processes, etc.) be very selective about which documents you use. It's especially important to delete references to confidential information, even if you've already left the organization. Exercising poor judgment can get you in trouble. You'll raise your prospective employer's suspicions about your ability to protect their organization's privacy. And you may even face possible legal action brought by your current or former employer.

Smart Move #114: Approach Questionable Situations Systematically

When you encounter a situation that makes you uncomfortable, approach it as systematically as possible. This is true whether you're directly involved or just observing the situation. In either case, you need to realize that many of these situations are ambiguous and that there are many legitimate reactions to them.

First, define the problem. Ask yourself: What specifically was said or done to me or someone else in my presence that made me uncomfortable? Try to identify specific words and/or actions that sparked your discomfort. The more specific you get, the better you'll be able to decide what to do about it. Writing your observations down is a very good idea.

Second, review your options. Ask yourself: What are my choices? There are three general things you can do in a questionable situation: Ignore it; confront it, or monitor it.

Naturally, you can decide to pretend the situation never happened (or is happening) and just get on with your daily business.

Another option is to address the situation in some way. For example, you could anonymously report the situation to your organization's ethics hotline or human resources personnel. You could speak with the person who caused the problem directly, or you could ask your manager or someone else in authority to intervene.

Still another possibility is to monitor the situation. Instead of dismissing it or taking action immediately, you could hang back and see how it unfolds. For example, you may suspect that you've witnessed a colleague engaging in unethical behavior, but you're not 100 percent sure. Document what you've witnessed as soon as possible. Then wait and see if it happens again. You may be able to better evaluate the situation if you observe a pattern of repeated incidents.

Third, consider the consequences of each option. Ask yourself: What would the likely outcome be if I ignored, addressed, or monitored the situation? Think about any previous, similar situations you've encountered and how they turned out. What did you or the person dealing with them do? Was the outcome favorable? If so, why? If not, why not?

Fourth, factor in your comfort level. Ask yourself: If I do x, can I live with the likely outcome? You may be fairly certain that following a specific course of action will resolve the problem. But you may not feel comfortable taking that action—or with the consequences of it.

Fifth, get some help if you need it. Ask yourself, "Do I need some advice from a more experienced professional? In ambiguous situations, it's understandable to feel confused. It's common to need some support and guidance. It's best to consult with individuals who aren't directly involved in the situation both to gain objectivity and to protect your confidentiality. For example, former professors or advisors, mentors, parents, clergy, and friends may be good choices for you.

Sixth, set a deadline for taking action. Ask yourself, "What's a realistic amount of time for me to devote to deciding what to do and doing it?" You could spend twenty-four hours a day analyzing and struggling with what to do and when to do it. It's vital that you give yourself deadlines for these two things, or else you'll let the situation take over your life and zap your energy.

PART II

How To Get Ahead

CHAPTER 3

Marketing Yourself

Work Smart IQ Quiz #3

Review each item below and decide if it's a work smart myth or a work smart reality. In the space before each statement, put an "M" if you think it's a myth and an "R" if you think it's a reality. Then check your responses with the correct answers at the end of the quiz.

_____ **1.** To advance your career, you'll need to play varied roles.

_____ **2.** When you're fairly well-established in your career, you don't really need a mentor.

_____ **3.** You're most likely to achieve your career goals if they are concrete, measurable, and realistic.

_____ **4.** Writing down your accomplishments as you go is only a smart move for people with poor memories.

_____ 5. Your manager controls the outcome of your performance review.

_____ 6. When it's your turn to speak at a staff meeting, make sure you share lots of details about the current status of your projects.

_____ 7. State the purpose of your memo up front.

_____ 8. Alternating between taking credit for things and letting others take it is important. It will show that you know how to work both independently and as a team player.

_____ 9. Networking is an inherently exploitative, insincere practice.

_____ 10. You should start developing a network of connections inside and outside of your organization when you need to make a job or career change.

Answers: (1)-R, (2)-M, (3)-R, (4)-M, (5)-M, (6)-M, (7)-R, (8)-R, (9)-M, (10)-M

RESPONSIBILITY

CHALLENGE: DETERMINING WHOSE IT IS

Greg's father, Dan, couldn't understand why Greg kept moving from one company to another every few years to get more experience and increase his pay. Dan criticized Greg for not making a commitment to one organization. Dan told Greg how he had worked for the same company for forty years. He had been a loyal employee and his organization had rewarded him with regular promotions and pay increases. Being part of a company that was like "one big family," Greg's father felt a consistent sense of job security. Greg tried to explain that things have changed, but he and his father couldn't seem to agree on this issue.

Holly worked for a very busy manager with a hands-off style. Her manager trusted Holly and the rest of her department to work with minimal supervision. Holly liked this management style and was very committed to her job. But Holly thought that having a lot of autonomy meant that she shouldn't bother her manager in between reviews with questions about how to be a better employee. At Holly's first performance review, her manager told her that she expected her to seek feedback and to use it in order to improve her performance on a regular basis.

TAKING CONTROL

Unlike your parents, you can't count on an organization to reward your loyalty and hard work with guaranteed, life-long employment. The buzzword for advancing your career has changed from paternalism to self-management. It's your responsibility to manage your career and make sure that you're on track. This sometimes means going from one organization to the next, like Greg chose to do. For more information on why it's okay to make a change in today's work world, see chapter 6.

Managing your career is especially important given the rising trends of telecommuting, smaller organizations, and self-employment. If you're one of the many workers who is working at home, part-or full-time, for a medium or small organization, or is self-employed, you know that there's no centralized, mega-structure watching out for your best interests. It's up to you to make things happen.

Even in a medium or large organization, your manager may or may not give you enough information about how to steer your career down the right path. Some managers take a very active role in helping you develop your skills and guide your career development. Others, like Holly's, are too busy, uninterested, or unskilled in how to coach you in this process. Either way, there are several smart moves that can help you take control of your career. We'll discuss each of them in detail throughout this chapter. For starters, though, it's important to think of each strategy as a part of your main job; "Career Manager."

Smart Move #115: Mimic the Head of Your Organization

Surround yourself with smart individuals, each with expertise in a specific, relevant area. These individuals will serve as mentors, or surrogate career counselors, and help you make informed decisions over time.

Smart Move #116: Become an Architect and a Strategic Planner

To set goals that make sense for your career progression, you need to play both of these roles. In your capacity as an architect, you'll develop flexible blueprints for mapping out your career development. And, like a strategic planner, you'll consider your short- and long-term options and how they relate to your goals to determine what direction to take.

Smart Move #117: Act Like an Accountant

Keep track of your accomplishments on an ongoing basis. You can record the revenue you've generated by tallying your achievements as career revenue.

Smart Move #118: Think Like a Film Critic and a Negotiator

In these capacities you can maximize your performance review process. The film critic in you can review the work you've done since your last review, articulating the strengths and weaknesses of your performance. As a negotiator, you can use this self-evaluation in your review to demonstrate why you deserve a compensation increase.

Smart Move #119: Be Your Own PR Coordinator

Before meetings, decide what to highlight about your projects when it's your turn to speak. Emphasize your accomplishments in project status memos. In these ways, you can promote yourself without coming off like an egomaniac.

Smart Move #120: Adopt the Mindset of a Politician

All effective politicians get in the habit of giving others credit as an integral part of everything they say and write. Advancing your career requires that you acknowledge that you're not operating in a vacuum. You'll get farther faster by recognizing others' contributions along the way.

Smart Move #121: Follow the Lead of a Talk Show Producer

Identify the people inside and outside of your organization who would be valuable contacts for you. Arrange to meet with them, in person if possible. Cultivate professional relationships with them so that they become professional resources in the future.

Our smart moves throughout the rest of the topics in this chapter—mentors, goals, accomplishment logs, performance reviews, campaigns, credit, and networking for connections—will show you more ways to market yourself effectively.

MENTORS

CHALLENGE: GOING IT ALONE

After two years with his company, Ted got promoted from his entry-level position to an associate-level position. Excited to finally have more responsibility and a new manager, Ted approached his new position with enthusiasm. He was disappointed when his new manager didn't make an effort to get to know him or ask about his goals. Since Ted's previous manager had an easygoing disposition and took a keen interest in his career development, he didn't know how to handle the situation.

Sally, Roy, Paul, and Joanne were all recent college grads who worked at ACME, Inc. The organization rolled out a new mentoring program and encouraged all of its young professionals to participate. Sally resisted because she was afraid that it would require too much work to keep the mentor-student relationship going. Roy wasn't interested, because he feared that what he told his mentor would get back to his manager. Paul said no, too, because he was concerned that his mentor would try to get the inside scoop on his department. Joanne didn't participate, because she was uncomfortable with the idea that the relationship would be one-sided. She didn't want to be beholden to anyone, or to answer to anyone other than her manager.

GETTING A MENTOR

At any point in your career, you, like Ted, may find yourself working for someone who isn't accessible or helpful about passing on their professional wisdom. If this happens, you're not doomed to muddle through alone. One option is to find and develop a relationship with a mentor. A mentor is someone who is more advanced in your field and can advise you about how to advance. A more experienced professional can be especially helpful when you have to make decisions about your career direction, on the job issues, and new responsibilities. This person can provide you with insights that will help you identify what you want to do and how to do it. It's understandable to have some reservations about participating in a mentoring relationship. But there are easy ways to address Sally, Roy, Paul, and Joanne's concerns, as we'll explain next.

Smart Move #122: Go Get 'Em

You may find a mentor within your organization, through continuing education, professional associations, or networking. A prospective mentor may approach you and take it upon himself to offer guidance. Or, if you suspect that an individual may be a suitable mentor, you may initiate contact by seeking his advice on a specific issue. This incident may evolve into a longer-term professional relationship.

Finding a Mentor Exercise

Directions: Even if your organization doesn't have a formal mentoring program, or if you don't want to participate in it, you can still develop a relationship with a mentor. Use the categories below to brainstorm some candidates you may want to approach or with whom you'd like to enhance an existing, informal mentoring relationship.

Former managers and colleagues:

College, graduate school, or other continuing education professors and advisors:

College, graduate school, or other continuing education alumni/ae:

Professional association members:

Church, synagogue, or other religious organization leaders or counselors:

Extended family members:

Neighbors/Acquaintances/Friends of friends:

Others:

Smart Move #123: Make It a Partnership

Whichever mentoring scenario unfolds, the relationship should be strictly professional and mutually consensual. Both you and your mentor must willingly agree to engage in this relationship and, together, determine how you'll maintain it. If you're worried (like Sally was) that it will be too much work, consider that there are no set rules about how often you meet or talk on the phone, which professional issues you focus on, or how long your mentoring relationship lasts.

Smart Move #124: Keep What You Discuss To Yourself

It should be made clear, however, that what you discuss remains confidential. This is especially important if your mentor works for the same organization as you. It's also vital that you and your mentor respect each other's boundaries. One or both of you may feel uncomfortable talking about certain people, topics, or incidents. In these cases, respect the limits as you would in any other relationship. Concerns such as Paul's, about feeling pressured to reveal inside information about his department, should be moot points.

Smart Move #125: "Pay Back" Your Mentor

If you're concerned about reciprocity like Joanne, realize that many people become mentors because they've benefited from these relationships themselves and want to give that experience to someone else. Your mentor may even address your concern by encouraging you to become a mentor to someone else at some point. Also, you can give to your mentor directly by showing appreciation for her time and insight. For example, you can periodically take her to lunch, give her a card, or tell her how much you value your mentoring relationship. On a regular basis, you can also show your mentor that you respect him by following his lead about the limits of your relationship. Then you can minimize the possibility of being too demanding or alienating your mentor.

---

5 Ways To Ruin Your Relationship With Your Mentor

1. Insist on turning your professional relationship into a friendship.
2. Intentionally discuss individuals or events that your mentor doesn't want to talk about.
3. Share with others private information that your mentor shares with you.
4. Neglect to acknowledge your mentor's support and guidance.
5. Take advantage of your mentoring relationship by calling, e-mailing, or dropping in on her whenever you want or need to get some help.

GOALS

Challenge: Knowing Where You're Going

Eric was very ambitious. He knew that to get ahead he had to keep track of where he'd been and where he wanted to go. He made a flexible blueprint for his career development. He regularly set goals like, "Sometime in the next few years I want to move up to a higher level position in my field," or "Next chance I get, I really want to learn how to improve my computer skills." Eric's intentions were good and his drive was strong, but he kept having trouble achieving his goals.

Serena set realistic, concrete, short-term goals for herself every quarter of the year. She recorded them in her organizer and broke them down into action steps with deadlines. But each quarter she had around twenty short-term goals on her list. Each goal had between five and ten steps. Serena spent so much time taking small bites out of her many goals that she only achieved one or two minor ones. She was disappointed in herself and couldn't figure out what she was doing wrong.

DEFINING AND REDEFINING YOUR CAREER GOALS

Setting career goals for yourself is a difficult, ongoing process. It's easy to make the mistake of either being too vague, like Eric, or too ambitious, like Serena. There are likely to be some formal opportunities to set goals, such as annual performance reviews. These discussions give you a chance to define your goals for the upcoming year with your manager's input. Regardless of whether or not you have formal performance reviews, it's critical that you set goals for yourself on a regular basis (annually, biannually, or quarterly).

Smart Move #126: Start Big

When you sit down to define your career goals, keep in mind that you can start with the big-picture and then figure out how your current job fits into your goal trajectories. First make a list of concrete, measurable things that you want to achieve in the next three months to four years. If you set goals that are too vague, you won't know when you've achieved them. Examples of measurable goals are: "Take three classes on topics a, b, and c,"; "Develop skills a, y, and z,"; "Get promoted to the next level." Make your list as long as you want. Don't worry about paring it down right away. Write your list of prospective goals in the space below:

1.

2.

3.

4.

5.

6.

7.

8.

9.

10.

Smart Move #127: Divide Your Short- and Long-term Goals

Now go down your list of prospective goals. Determine which are short-term and which are long-term. A short-term goal is one that you could realistically accomplish within about three to six months. A long-term goal is one that you could possibly achieve within one to four years. Keep in mind, though, that "short-term" and "long-term" are somewhat subjective terms. Depending on your career path, you may want to change "short-term" to mean six months to a year, and "long-term" to extend beyond four years. Label the short-term goals with an "s" and the long-term goals with an "l."

You might label the examples above as follows:

(s)   Take three classes on a, b, and c topics.

(s)   Develop x, y, and z skills.

(l)   Get promoted to the next level.

Smart Move #128: Make the Final Cut

The third step is to select the most important goals for the final cut. Keep the number of goals realistic as well. Trying to achieve too much will only make you spread yourself too thin. Be honest with yourself and go for quality over quantity.

Short-term Goals	Long-term Goals
1.	1.
2.	2.
3.	3.

Smart Move #129: Develop an Action Plan

Next, you need to establish action steps and timelines for achieving these goals. Create an action plan, such as the one below, to help organize your thoughts.

Short-term Goal #1: _____   Time Frame: _____

Action Steps:

1.   Time Frame: _____

2.   Time Frame: _____

3.   Time Frame: _____

4.   Time Frame: _____

5.   Time Frame: _____

Short-term Goal #2 _____   Time Frame: _____

Action Steps

1.   Time Frame: _____

2.   Time Frame: _____

3.   Time Frame: _____

4.   Time Frame: _____

5.   Time Frame: _____

Short-term Goal #3: _____   Time Frame: _____

Action Steps:

1   Time Frame: _____

2.   Time Frame: _____

3.   Time Frame: _____

4.   Time Frame: _____

5.   Time Frame: _____

Long-term Goal #1:_____   Time Frame: _____

Action Steps:

1.   Time Frame: _____

2.   Time Frame: _____

3.   Time Frame: _____

4.   Time Frame: _____

5.   Time Frame: _____

Long-term Goal #2 _____   Time Frame: _____

Action Steps:

1.   Time Frame: _____

2.   Time Frame: _____

3.   Time Frame: _____

4.   Time Frame: _____

5.   Time Frame: _____

Long-term Goal #3:_____   Time Frame: _____

Action Steps:

1.   Time Frame: _____

2.   Time Frame: _____

3.   Time Frame: _____

4.   Time Frame: _____

5.   Time Frame: _____

For more information on breaking goals down into manageable steps, see the timing section in chapter 8.

ACCOMPLISHMENT LOGS

CHALLENGE: DEMONSTRATING YOUR VALUE

Jeff applied for a job at an organization. He did all of the right things—researched the organization, targeted his resume and cover letter, landed an interview, and followed up afterwards. He made it to the final round of the selection process, but lost out to another applicant. When the hiring manager called to tell him the news, Jeff inquired about what would have made him the top candidate for the position. The hiring manager said that it was a tough call, because Jeff and the winning applicant were almost equally qualified for the position. The deciding factor was that the other applicant had some training experience. Jeff was surprised, since the hiring manager had only mentioned that training might become part of the job in the future. At the time it had seemed insignificant, so Jeff had concentrated on playing up the skills that matched the core requirements for the position. He had forgotten that he had done some training earlier in his career, and the hiring manager had no idea that Jeff had any such experience. The other candidate had presented evidence of this ultimately crucial point. Ironically, Jeff suspected that he had more substantial training experience than the candidate who got the job offer.

Amanda was feeling kind of down about her job. She hadn't felt stimulated or that she'd made a major contribution in a long time. Due to a recent merger and pending restructuring, her company had been in a holding pattern for months. Amanda was one of many employees who were maintaining the status quo until the senior management could chart a new direction and budget. Given the changes in her organization, she was left unsure of both how to measure her value and how to reinvent herself.

LOGGING YOUR ACCOMPLISHMENTS

Knowing you're doing a great job won't move your career forward. You've got to remember precisely what you did and when you did it in order to promote yourself to others. And you'll have ample opportunity to promote yourself—during a performance review with your manager, at meetings, in inter-office memos, when you update your resume, and during your next job interview. You may think it's no problem to remember your big accomplishments, but when you're really busy you tend to forget important accomplishments. An achievement that seems relatively minor at the time, like Jeff's training experience, may be just what you need to land a promotion, or another job later. Besides, keeping track of your achievements as you progress in your career will enable you to give yourself pats on the back when you're feeling like Amanda was.

Being able to see your success patterns over time will help you set more precise goals. For example, if you've made lots of contributions on your own during the last year, you may want to try to make more as part of a team. Or if you've achieved most of your triumphs in one or two areas within your field, you may want to try to expand into other, related areas to round yourself out. The opposite may also be true; you may be a terrific generalist now, but want to become a specialist in one area.

Smart Move #130: Maintain a Consistent Log

One of the easiest ways to keep track of what you're up to is to keep an accomplishment log. Start the log every time you begin a new job, and update it every time you complete another project. Write your accomplishments down as soon after they happen as possible so that they're fresh in your mind. This will be less of a hassle than playing catch-up later on.

Smart Move #131: Be Discreet

Whether you keep a handwritten log in a notebook or on your computer, make sure that it's confidential. It's better to maintain your accomplishment log at home, rather than at work. When ideas occur to you at work, jot them down and bring them home.

Smart Move #132: Base Your Format on Key Information

You can format your log in many different ways. Whatever way you choose, include the following key information: date(s) of the accomplishment, role in the accomplishment (e.g., team leader, project manager, broker, etc.), and a brief description of what you accomplished. In the description, think about the challenge you faced, your behavior, and the outcome. Then describe what you did as specifically as possible. Follow the bullet point format you would use when drafting a resume, starting each line with a power verb and quantifying your accomplishments as much as possible.

Here's an example of an accomplishments log for you to use as a guideline:

Sample Log
Accomplishment #1:
Date(s): Month/Date/Year
Your Role: Position Title or Special Role (e.g., Team Leader, Project Manager, etc.)

Description of What You Achieved:
-
-
-

Accomplishment #2:
Date(s): Month/Date/Year
Your Role: Position Title or Special Role (e.g., Team Leader, Project Manager, etc.)
Description of What You Achieved:
-
-
-

Accomplishment #3:
Date(s): Month/Date/Year
Your Role: Position Title or Special Role (e.g., Team Leader, Project Manager, etc.)
Description of What You Achieved:
-
-
-

PERFORMANCE REVIEWS

CHALLENGE: HANDLING THE PROCESS

Brian's manager invited him to help pick coworkers who would provide feedback on his performance. Brian didn't give it much thought and suggested three colleagues who he'd worked with. When his manager gave him the composite feedback from these people, Brian was shocked to discover that the negative comments outnumbered the positive comments. His limited exposure to these people made it tough for them to provide substantial feedback, and what they did report was based on a few isolated incidents. Brian tried to explain this to his manager, who replied that he'd take Brian's reactions into consideration. His manager advised him to exercise more care about who he selects in the future.

At 4:30 p.m. on a Thursday, Ilyse returned to her desk after a meeting to find a blank self-evaluation form for her upcoming performance review. On it was a note from her manager, instructing her to bring the completed form to her performance review at 9:30

the following morning. Ilyse tried to find her manager to request more time to fill out the form and discovered that he had already left for an evening event.

Ethan came to his performance review prepared to discuss his goals for the following year with his manager. His manager explained her vision and priorities for the organization and department. He listened carefully and then reviewed his career development goals with her. Instead of looking pleased, she frowned and took a long pause before responding to him. She asked him how he thought his individual goals might fit with the organization's needs. Ethan didn't respond directly. Instead, he re-emphasized what he wanted to get from the organization and how he wanted to get it.

Chip sat down in his manager's office for his performance review, prepared to spend at least a half-hour discussing his past performance and future goals. His manager, however, rushed through the discussion. She mechanically ran down the form and gave him both positive feedback and constructive criticism. She didn't back up her comments with examples. She didn't even stop in between categories to let him respond. Chip just figured that his turn would come when she was done. When she reached to the end of the form, she simply said a rhetorical, "Okay?" and directed him to the line at the bottom where he needed to sign. Before he could say anything, she hit the intercom button and asked her secretary to send the next person in. Chip was unhappy, but he didn't know what to do.

TAKING AN ACTIVE ROLE

Many organizations have their managers conduct performance reviews at regular intervals. In some workplaces, this happens at an employee's annual anniversary with the organization. At others, performance reviews are done at the same time every year to coincide with decisions about salary increases and/or bonuses. Some organizations even mandate reviews every six months. There are still other organizations that don't provide formal performance reviews at all. Whether or not you have a formal review scheduled, you need to solicit feedback about the quality of your work and to plan for the future on an ongoing basis.

Regardless of the frequency, performance reviews are a key opportunity for you to advance your career. The two primary goals of the performance review process are for you and your manager to evaluate the quality of your job performance since your last review and to plan for your career development. What follows are some strategies to avoid the problems that Brian, Ilyse, Ethan, and Chip ran into.

Smart Move #133: Select Reviewers Who Know You Well

Although the format of these reviews varies widely between organizations, there are still a few common smart moves you can use to make the most of your review. First, your manager may approach the review process by gathering information about your performance from yor colleagues (superiors, peers, subordinates, and possibly outside clients). In this case, you may have input into selecting your appraisers. Carefully consider those you've worked with closely who can consequently give your manager specific feedback about your performance. The more familiar your appraisers are with your work, the better it is for you. Others' comments about your strengths will carry a lot of weight in your favor, and their suggestions about your areas for development will be easier for you to respond to, if necessary.

Smart Move #134: Understand Your Assessment Rating System

Another, more typical component of a performance review is a self-appraisal. You're likely to have the chance to rate your performance, outline some goals for moving forward, and then share your perspective with your manager. Your manager will probably give you a blank copy of the performance review form that he use to evaluate you and ask you to complete it before meeting with him.

It's important that you understand your particular performance assessment rating system. For example, your organization's system may be based on a numerical rating system whereby you assign a number rating to each category that you're being evaluated on. Let's say your rating key goes from 1-4 (1 being the highest rating and 4 being the lowest). You go through the form and assign a number to skills categories such as problem-solving, communication, and teamwork. Or, your organization may use letters, phrases, or combinations of these ratings to designate how well you meet the expectations of your job. If you have any questions about how your rating system works or what the options mean, ask your manager before you complete the form.

Smart Move #135: Get a Self-Appraisal Deadline and Do It Right

Make sure that you establish a time frame for completing your self-appraisal with your manager. Since reviews may be conducted at a busy time of year, your manager may give you your form at the last minute. To avoid getting caught off-guard, ask your manager when you can expect to receive your self-appraisal form so that you can complete it thoroughly. When you get the form, ask whether you'll be submitting it before your performance review discussion or bringing it to the session. Either way, give it a lot of time and attention. How seriously you take your self-appraisal will further reflect on your overall job performance.

Smart Move #136: Pull Achievements and Goals From Your Log

Use your accomplishments log to make your performance review preparation easier. Review your log for any relevant achievements during the performance period. Next to each skills category on your appraisal form there are probably blanks for comments. Use these spaces to back up your self-ratings with examples of your accomplishments. Without evidence, your ratings are not as powerful.

You can also use your log to help with the goal-setting part of your appraisal. Reflect on where you've been and where you want to be. You may not be aware of what your manager has in mind for you, so be certain to keep your goals realistic. You'll have a chance to refine these goals when you have your performance review meeting. Do the best you can and try to match what you want for your career development with the organization's needs and priorities. Be creative about how you may accomplish this. It's an ideal opportunity to pitch some mutually beneficial ideas to your manager. Also, remember to state your proposed goals in concrete, measurable terms, just like you did in your accomplishments log.

Smart Move #137: Make Your Review Discussion Work for You

When you actually sit down with your manager to discuss your performance, she may or may not have already given you a written copy of her appraisal of you. Keep in mind that your discussion should be a positive, constructive one. You need to keep an open mind and demonstrate that you're responsive to comments about both your strengths and weaknesses.

This can be especially difficult in an ultra-competitive organization where high ratings are scarce. For example, some companies tie performance reviews to salary increases and bonus pools. This means that each department head has a certain amount of money he can allocate to each employee. This system requires that department managers rank other department members relative to one another—and there's only room for one top performer who receives the highest ranking possible. It's like grading on a curve in school. Everyone else is ranked relative to the top person. Even if you don't work for a company that operates like this, keep in mind that you'll be evaluated against the highest possible performance standards.

Smart Move #138: Turn Around a Rude Reviewer

It's also possible that your manager may not handle your performance review to your satisfaction. For instance, he may talk at you at top speed, whipping through his comments in thirty seconds flat. Or he may give you lots of positive and negative feedback in vague terms without providing examples to illustrate his comments. He may not solicit your input or give you a chance to ask clarifying questions, raise your concerns, or disagree with his points. None of these scenarios are acceptable.

Without becoming defensive or aggressive, tell your manager that you'd like to address some issues. If he's still not responsive to your needs, you don't have to sign the final performance review form until you have a chance to work it out. Your signature usually doesn't indicate that you agree with what is there, it only means that you understand it. But you still have a right to ask your manager to modify his review based on your discussion or at least to attach your addendum to it. And, regardless of whether or not you're satisfied, you should get a copy of the full, final review for your records.

Smart Move #139: Follow Up In Between Reviews

After your performance review is over, you can't just file it away and forget about it until next time. Follow up is key. Go over your goals between then and your next performance review. Break these goals down into action steps and time frames. Then follow your action plan and check in with your manager from time to time to see how you're doing.

Smart Move #140: Make the Best of a Bad Review

If you receive a performance review that says you're an unacceptably poor performer, your manager will establish some kind of performance "contract" with you. You'll probably be placed on probation for the next month or so. And you'll have to achieve very specific goals within prescribed periods of time in order to get off probation. If you fail to meet these goals, it's likely that you'll be fired.

This situation shouldn't come as a complete surprise to you. Your manager should tell you regularly when your work or behavior is substandard and how to remedy it. If the first time you hear really bad news is during your review, then your manager is doing something wrong. Sometimes managers are too nice or timid to tell their subordinates what's wrong when it happens. Other managers either don't want to spend the time or don't know how to discuss it. Still others just don't care. And it's understandable if you feel ashamed, embarrassed, angry, or some combination of these emotions.

CAMPAIGNS

CHALLENGE: PROMOTING YOUR ACCOMPLISHMENTS

Stan was a very thorough worker. He planned, executed, and followed up on projects under deadline pressure and always maintained an even temperament. He was modest, though, and depended upon others to let his manager know about his accomplishments. Since very few people took the time to sponsor Stan, his manager didn't really know how much of an asset he was to the company. Stan realized that this was slowing his career advancement down, but he wasn't comfortable touting himself to his manager.

At the end of Lara's departmental staff meetings, everyone regularly took turns sharing updates with the group. Lara always winged it and usually went into great detail about projects that others only gave highlights about. She also often asked for feedback on almost every outstanding issue, and believed that it was worth taking the group's time since they'd appreciate being asked for their advice.

Terry graduated from college with honors in English literature, and she prided herself on her writing skills. In her first job she continued to write the way she had in college. She favored long, metaphorical sentences over short direct ones. Terry's manager repeatedly returned her memos marked up with style corrections. Terry took it personally and got offended. She didn't understand why her writing was good enough to get her the job but wasn't good enough to use there.

USING STAFF MEETINGS AND MEMOS

Hard work plus diligence over time equals recognition and rewards for your efforts. Right? Not necessarily. Just as the era of paternalistic employers has ended, so has the myth that all it takes to manage your career is to bury yourself in your work and do a good job. Like Stan, you may not want to deal with making sure others know what you're up to. Or, like Lara, you may like promoting yourself too much. Or, like Terry, you may think your communication style is appropriate when it's not. Using staff meetings and memos to promote your accomplishments tactfully will help you make your career successful. There are different ways you can accomplish this without feeling uncomfortable, going overboard, or deviating from accepted communication styles.

Smart Move #141: Identify Your Weak Spots

Meeting Bloopers And Memo Blunders Exercise

Directions: Use the checklists below to identify which meeting and memo skills you need to work on correcting. Put a check next to all bloopers and blunders that you can claim as yours.

Meeting Bloopers

_____ Editorializing about the current status of your projects.

_____ Giving the same updates to different audiences.

_____ Soliciting feedback from people who can't help or who shouldn't be aware of certain issues.

_____ Planning meetings that don't creatively showcase your areas of expertise or relevant interests.

Memo Blunders

_____ Deleting the basics.

_____ Ignoring transitions.

_____ Skipping the purpose of the memo.

_____ Writing long, dense paragraphs.

_____ Making only vague, generalized references to the outcome of a project and to your accomplishments.

_____ Using a formal tone for an informal memo or vice versa.

_____ Writing in passive voice.

_____ Ending without wrapping it up.

_____ Circulating it without spell-checking or grammar-checking it first.

Smart Move #142: Make Your Meeting Updates Selective and Direct

One way you can market yourself as a valuable employee is to make the most of staff meetings. In many organizations you may have a regular staff meeting with your manager and department colleagues on a weekly, bimonthly, or monthly basis. Regardless of how frequently or infrequently you meet, make sure you prepare for these meetings by reviewing the status of your current projects.

The agendas for your department staff meetings will usually follow a predictable pattern, so determine how to prepare and what to highlight beforehand. When it's your turn to share what's going on with your work, you can report what phases of projects (or entire projects) are completed, update the group about how you've resolved certain problems, and solicit input about outstanding issues. As always, use your discretion about how much talking to do—especially when it's self-promoting. A good way to minimize your risk of coming across as self-absorbed or verbose is to stick to the facts rather than editorializing at length.

Smart Move #143: Tailor Your Meeting Updates to Your Audience

Remember to select what you report based on your audience. For example, it's not necessarily appropriate to go into detail about problems or their resolutions with people who weren't in the loop throughout the process. On the other hand, if your department is sharing problem-solving strategies for common issues or if you all have worked on a project together, it may be relevant to give others some insight into what's up and why.

Smart Move #144: Ask Only for Appropriate Input During Meetings

Similarly, when it comes to soliciting input from others, keep in mind who can really help you out and what the protocol for problem-solving is in your department. For example, you may need to run a problem by your manager first, as both a matter of professional courtesy and to determine whether you can share this problem openly with the whole department.

Smart Move #145: Be a Creative Meeting Leader

Another type of department staff meeting involves rotating leadership. In this case, every department member takes responsibility for developing and facilitating the agenda for a particular meeting, either alone or in teams. This type of staff meeting is an ideal opportunity for you to demonstrate how you can make a unique contribution to your department.

Consider how your strengths and interests match the current needs of your department. Then plan a fun, informative meeting that will engage your colleagues and showcase your talents. For example, you can invite a guest speaker (or speakers) from another department who will address a key, specialized area of knowledge, plan an interactive learning exercise on a topic such as team-building, or develop a slide presentation on a current trend in your field. By taking a creative approach to both the topic and format of the meeting, you'll show that you're in sync with the department's needs and a valuable asset to the team.

Smart Move #146: Remember Your Memo Header Basics

Using follow-up memos is another effective way to market yourself. Even if you typically give your manager project updates verbally, you can leave a paper trail during and after a project. Use e-mail or a hard copy memo to highlight key milestones along the way and summarize your accomplishments after your project is completed.

Some organizations or departments use memo templates to produce memos. These templates prompt you to enter the heading information into a standard format for your workplace. There are so many variations on the order and aesthetics of this format that it's most important to pay attention to what others do and follow their lead. Remember to always include the basic information:

- HEADING (MEMO or MEMORANDUM) at the top
- TO: line
- FROM: line
- RE: line
- DATE: line
- CC: line (if necessary)

Smart Move #147: Divide and Conquer Memo Content

Since memos are like business letters, most often the text is placed flush left, rather than indented. Because it's a memo, you can put subheadings between paragraphs or sets of paragraphs if it makes it easier to read. Adding underlined, bold subheadings such as PURPOSE and NEXT STEPS is usually appropriate when you're sending a memo about a project plan or notes from a meeting. Often, though, your memo will stand alone without headings as long as your transitions are smooth and the memo is relatively brief.

Smart Move #148: Open Your Memos with the Point

Just as when you write a resume, it's best to keep your memos focused. Make sure you state your purpose upfront. First sentences like, "I'm writing to inform you that..." are awkward and make your memo sound like junk mail. Cut to the chase. Pretend you're phoning someone with important news and write it this way. For example, "There will be a meeting on the 24th to discuss..." or "Now that we've completed Phase 2 of the Excaliber Project. . . ."

Smart Move #149: Write Your Memos Concisely and Clearly

Save long, metaphorical sentences for your first novel. Don't try to impress your coworkers with big words and generalized comments. You'll only end up sounding immature and awkward. Write like you speak, censoring any slang or poor grammar, and back up your points with concrete examples and detail. You want to avoid receiving a barrage of inquiries later on. After all, the point of the memo is to help clarify any confusion about the issue. Sometimes using bullets or indented numbers within a paragraph can be effective.

Smart Move #150: Quantify Your Accomplishments in Memos

When you discuss your accomplishments, and those of your coworkers, remember to quantify them as much as possible. Again, it's the same principle as when you're writing a resume. You want to show how your contribution has affected the bottom line at your company. For instance, it's more persuasive to write that your efforts increased sales 45 percent than just to say that you took an innovative approach to a marketing campaign.

If it's too difficult or premature to fully quantify an achievement, then document the outcome as specifically as possible. Let's say that you introduced a streamlined, two-day training program for new employees that was a huge success. You're not really sure exactly how to convey that this program has enabled new hires to perform their jobs better, but you can point out, for example, that it reduced the number of days that Training Department members and new hires were involved in training. The program thereby saved the company money because the in-house training facilities weren't tied up, the material costs were lowered, and employees weren't away from their jobs for as long as before.

Smart Move #151: Customize the Tone of Your Memos

The tone of each memo will vary based on the purpose. In general, though, it's better to err on the side of formality. This doesn't mean using stilted language. It just means that you're not writing a letter to a friend. It's a business document and should reflect that fact. The best memos are similar to good speeches. They are professional, but sound natural and reflect the voice of the writer.

Smart Move #152: Use Active Voice in Your Memos

Another related element concerns passive versus active voice. Your memo will be powerful and effective if you use the latter. Active voice: "I organized the meeting." Passive voice: "The meeting was organized by me." Many people accidentally slip into passive voice mid-memo. Passive voice is poor grammar. More importantly, it makes you sound like a follower rather than a leader.

Smart Move #153: Wrap It Up at the End of Your Memos

It may be tempting to just stop writing when you've said what you want to say. But then your memo will sound like you abruptly ended a conversation with someone. The best way to end a memo is to include a brief wrap-up. Usually, this will consist of a preview of what's next. For example, you may say, "Our next meeting will be on January 3rd, in Conference Room B, at 3:00 p.m.," or "I will give you the final version of the documentation for the Excaliber Project by the end of next week." It's also courteous to reiterate that you're available to clarify any aspect of the memo. Say, "If you have any questions or comments, please let me know," or "In the meantime, you can contact me at...." Sometimes, in a final memo concerning a project, it's appropriate to thank a person or group for their support. For instance, "Thank you again for your time and valuable input," or "I really appreciate your participation in this project. It has helped to make it a success." Whatever you say, make it sincere and appropriate to the situation.

Smart Move #154: Proof Your Memos Carefully

As with any work documents, proofread your memo for spelling and grammar mistakes before you circulate it. When you're on a tight deadline, it's easy to skip these steps. But small mistakes will distract your reader from the content and make you look inept. If you feel like you can't be objective or are weak at spelling and grammar, use your computer spell check and grammar check functions. Remember, though, that spell check doesn't catch synonyms. That's why it's a good idea to have a good proofreader look it over. If you get stuck doing it yourself, reading your memo out loud is an effective way to catch mistakes.

CREDIT

CHALLENGE: BALANCING TAKING IT AND GIVING IT

Peter did a great job and knew it. He was confident in the quality of his work and wasn't afraid to show it. He consistently took advantage of opportunities to market himself on the job, especially during staff meetings. Peter frequently made comments taking credit for his ideas and accomplishments that started with "I": "I thought of a cool new idea to market this product," or "I finished that project without a hitch." He said "I" 99 percent of the time, even when referring to team efforts. He thought he was cleverly plugging himself, which he saw as the best way to advance his career. When his colleagues seemed irritated by his comments, he figured they were just jealous that he had beaten them to the punch.

Aileen was known for her timely, comprehensive memos that updated other team members on the status of current projects. The others really appreciated that she kept track of the issues and made sure that everyone was in the loop. But they secretly didn't like the fact that she tended to take more of the credit than she gave. While Aileen's coworkers saw her memos as genuine efforts to inform everyone, they also couldn't help but view them as veiled advertisements for Aileen. Because no one confronted her, Aileen was unaware of their feelings. She didn't understand why they salted their praise with sarcastic asides. She just wrote off the kidding as part of the normal group dynamics of the team.

A Game of Give and Take

It's important to differentiate between individual achievements and those you achieve in conjunction with others. In memos and meetings alike, make sure you say "we" as much as you say "I." Knowing when to take credit and knowing when to give it is vital. It will also show that you know how to work both independently and as a team player. This will reflect well on you, since teamwork is an increasingly hot competency (see chapter 4, hot competencies section) in the most progressive, successful organizations. As you can see from the Peter and Aileen scenarios above, knowing when and how to take credit is an especially important skill. In the smart moves that follow we suggest ways to take credit, give it, and balance the two.

Smart Move #155: Take the Credit You Deserve

When you truly deserve credit for accomplishing something, then take it. Don't play it down. If you don't let others know what you've done, then who will? If you tend to get cocky and brag about or inflate your achievements, you'll alienate others.

Often times you'll achieve something in the context of a group project. You may think it's difficult for you to identify your specific contributions in these situations, but it's still possible and valuable for you to put your work in the context of your coworker's work. It's in your best interest to point out that you were involved with specific phases of a particular project, such as developing, instituting, or maintaining it. Even if you codeveloped, coinstituted, and comaintained something, it still counts in your favor as a contribution. So don't overlook projects that you did with others.

In fact, you should emphasize accomplishments that illustrate your teamwork skills. For instance, it's significant if you played a role as a liaison between two or more departments, were the project leader for a specific project, or served on a division-wide or organization-wide task force. In these cases, remember to mention what you accomplished in terms of how successfully you functioned as part of a group. Successfully facilitating communication between different people, motivating a team to complete high quality work that meets deadlines, providing and taking constructive criticism, and functioning as a well-respected, active member of a diverse team are among the skills that will prove that you're a valuable employee.

Smart Move #156: Highlight What You Learn and Its Future Applications

Skills or knowledge that you gained by working on a project are also key things to include in a follow-up memo to your manager. This information is important for two reasons. First, it demonstrates that you took the initiative to learn what you had to in order to get the job done. Second, it shows what relevant, transferable skills you can contribute to future projects. Your manager will then perceive you as a distinctive, valuable employee—one who is proactive, has a strong work ethic, and is committed to ongoing learning.

Smart Move #157: Send Credit Memos to the Right People

Exercise careful judgment when sending a copy or copies of such a memo to coworkers besides your manager. One way to prevent yourself from appearing to be a grandstander is to send one version of an update memo that covers the key points for those who need to know about the status of a project. Stick to the facts and let your self-promotion be more subtle. The fact that your memo is well written, concise, and timely will show that you have your act together. Then draft a second, more detailed version of the memo, highlighting more of your contributions, and send it just to your manager.

Smart Move #158: Consolidate Your Credit Memos

Also, sending one detailed wrap-up memo to your manager at the end of a project is more effective than giving your manager multiple memos. One exception is if you work on a long-term project over several months. Then it may be appropriate to give your manager more frequent updates, especially to ensure that your manager will take your accomplishments into consideration during your performance review periods.

Smart Move #159: Include Coworkers' Contributions in Your Memo

It also makes you look good to recognize the contributions of others. Although the main purpose of a follow-up memo is to document the status of a project and your contributions to it, you can also include a brief mention of others' input. This is especially relevant if any of the people you're acknowledging also report to your manager or to someone else on the distribution list.

Smart Move #160: Know When to Give Others Special Recognition

In special cases, it may also be smart to write a separate memo to a colleague, cc'ing her supervisor (or the other way around). For example, if you were the project leader or in another position of authority, it's a professional gesture to recognize someone's outstanding work in this way. Just make the memo genuine, specific, and respectful. Some organizations run service awards programs on a monthly, quarterly, or yearly basis. Through such programs, you can nominate a colleague for a recognition award and give him credit in this way.

NETWORKING FOR CONNECTIONS

CHALLENGE: DEVELOPING CONNECTIONS

Jason wasn't into schmoozing. He thought that seeking out new people and making small talk was a waste of his valuable time. He tended to keep to himself and his circle of colleagues in his department. He really enjoyed his work, was good at it, and put in a lot of hours fulfilling his job requirements.

But after his first year on the job, he started to notice that some of his coworkers were finding out about desirable job opportunities before he was. They were also dealing better with the politics required to get projects started. He asked a few of his colleagues how they were getting all of these advantages. They explained to him about making connections, but Jason decided that it was just the luck of the draw, being in the right place at the right time. He didn't understand the value of connecting and decided to continue managing his career the same way as before.

NETWORKING IN AND OUT OF THE OFFICE

You can enhance your visibility by building a network. Unfortunately, Jason didn't know until it was too late that networking is not an inherently exploitative, insincere practice. When it's done right, networking (formally and informally making connections with key people inside and outside of your organization) is a mutually beneficial professional practice.

Smart Move #161: Make Inside Connections

Inside of your organization, develop professional relationships with key players in related areas. Volunteering to serve on cross-departmental task forces or eating lunch in a group with new acquaintances are two easy ways to get to know new colleagues.

Over time, you can share key information about what you're working on and how it's going. Exchanging information verbally is a comfortable, casual way to let people know about your accomplishments. You also benefit from these relationships in other ways. You'll learn more about current events in your organization, as well as about potential job opportunities first-hand. You'll build alliances with others that may prove useful when you need to get work information quickly or collaborate on projects together.

Smart Move #162: Connect Beyond Your Organization's Walls

Networking outside of your organization will further strengthen your promotional efforts. Since many up-and-coming, as well as senior-level professionals belong to professional associations, it's to your advantage to join a couple of the main ones in your field. You can find the best ones for you by checking out the Encyclopedia of Associations (see the Appendix for references) in your public library and asking more seasoned professionals what associations they belong to. Undergraduate and graduate school alumni/ae events are also good places to network.

Attend local as well as national professional association and alumni/ae events whenever possible and get to know others. You'll establish yourself as a committed, young professional in the eyes of others active in the field. In turn, they'll most likely praise your involvement and accomplishments to your organization's managers. Associations and alumni/ae groups usually breed tightly-knit professional networks of individuals who know and can help each other move ahead in their careers.

You can also use the resources of your college or graduate school to help you make connections. For example, you can contact your undergraduate college or graduate school's Alumni and Career Services Offices for networking contacts. One or both of these offices may provide you with computer printouts of alumni in your field of interest for a nominal fee. Often it's more comfortable and productive to contact alumni since you already have your school in common. Your school's faculty, administrators, and career counselors can also guide you in the right direction. (For more details about using your school for networking help, see chapter 8, transition resources section).

It's also worth the effort to network informally outside of work through friends and hobbies. You may be surprised at how many people who can affect your career development are accessible through your friends and activities. Friends are often happy to introduce each other to those with common career paths. And in your activities (at the gym, art class, etc.) you already have something in common to use as an icebreaker. By networking formally and informally both inside and outside work, you can expand your circle of influence and advance your career.

Smart Move #163: Expand Your Circle of Connections

Connections Exercise

Directions: Come up with at least five ways that you can expand your connections with key people inside of your organization (e.g., serving on a cross-departmental task force, eating lunch with a group of new acquaintances, etc.). Then list at least three professional associations that you could join to promote your networking efforts outside of your organization. Ask colleagues in your field for suggestions of key associations and check out *The Dictionary of Associations* at the library for more ideas.

Connecting Inside:

1.

2.

3.

4.

5.

Connecting Outside:

1.

2.

3.

4.

5.

Myths About Networking

1) *You have to know a million people.*
2) *You have to like making small talk.*
3) *You're imposing on other people.*
4) *You can only do it outside of your organization.*
5) *You can only benefit from it if you're job hunting right now.*

CHAPTER 4

Making Yourself
The Office "MVP"

WORK SMART IQ QUIZ #4

Review each item below and decide if it's a work smart myth or a work smart reality. In the space before each statement, put an "M" if you think it's a myth and an "R" if you think it's a reality. Then check your responses with the correct answers at the end of the quiz.

_____ **1.** Follow your instincts when you think a project is heading in the wrong direction.

_____ **2.** You're just too busy to manage your time and clutter better.

_____ **3.** It's not your responsibility to worry about when other people take their vacations.

_____ **4.** The best way to handle ambiguous comments or directives is to make assumptions.

5. Internal VIPs aren't necessarily the individuals who hold the highest titles or the longest tenure with the organization. They're the ones who have the most clout in terms of your work load.

6. You should protect your manager from surprises by informing her immediately of any issues that may involve or affect her.

7. You should prioritize specialized, "hard" skills over general, "soft" skills, like teamwork, risk-taking, critical thinking, and conflict resolution.

8. You need to find ways to maintain new skills or you'll lose them.

9. It's important to develop special skills that are unique and relevant, regardless of whether you enjoy them, if you want to stand out.

10. Different organizations define cost-effective in different ways.

Answers: (1)-R, (2)-M, (3)-M, (4)-M, (5)-R, (6)-R, (7)-M, (8)-R, (9)-M, (10)-R

PROACTIVITY

CHALLENGE: ANTICIPATING AND MEETING YOUR MANAGER'S NEEDS

Elaine sensed that she should check the latest journals in her field for more data on a project proposal that was due to a funding source in two weeks. But since she'd already done a thorough search the previous week, she dismissed her precautionary feeling as nervousness. The day after Elaine submitted her proposal, her manager told her that she should have checked the latest issue of the premier journal in her field. The lead article documented a discovery that significantly undermined the credibility of the proposal's angle.

Ben was sure he had the things he needed to meet his deadline with no problem. He'd always prided himself on having a great memory and rarely wrote things down, despite the fact that Ben kept everything in towering, cross-hatched piles on his desk. At the beginning of his deadline week, Ben was called into several emergency meetings about the project. In each meeting, the facilitator announced a few key dates and times for interim deadlines and follow-up meetings. Ben and his colleagues worked really late, and Ben was so tired that his super memory failed him. He mixed up most of the following day's deadline and meeting times. After yelling at Ben for screwing up, his manager came to his desk at the end of the day to retrieve a document that was past due. Ben was so unnerved that he accidentally knocked the huge pile it was in over, scattering papers that were in order all over the floor.

Kevin saw a bargain airfare advertised in the newspaper six months before the winter holidays. It was an unusually low fare and he really wanted to get away for a week in December. He called the airline and was lucky enough to get the last seat at the non-refundable, promotion rate. The next day at work, he bragged to his department about the great deal he got for vacation tickets. Instead of being happy for him, his coworkers asked him why he didn't check with them about the timing first. One coworker had to go to her sister's wedding for a couple of days that week. Another person had a business trip scheduled for the majority of that time. Kevin's manager reprimanded him for not checking with her first, and told him not to count on using his tickets.

Dina arrived at work to find a voice mail from her manager who was out of town at a meeting. Her manager told her that he would need a document prepared soon, so Dina should begin working on it. Dina assumed that "soon" meant in the next week or two. So she tackled her urgent projects and worked on this new assignment only a little over the next couple of days. When her manager returned three days later, he informed Dina that he needed the completed document the following day. Dina had to drop everything and frantically rush to get it done. In the meantime, she fell behind on other deadlines.

Reid typically corresponded with his colleague overseas by fax with no glitches. Once, though, he left something that his colleague needed in a few hours until the last minute. Reid figured that the time difference would give him plenty of time to finish it up and fax it over. At 2:00 a.m., he prepared the papers to fax, put them in the fax machine, and hit send. Understandably sleepy, Reid decided to go home, rather than wait to make sure the fax machine was operating properly. Just after he closed the door behind him, his fax indicated that it was unable to connect with the other machine because it wasn't on. Reid didn't discover this problem until nine o'clock that morning. By that time, his colleague had missed his deadline and was furious with Reid.

Naomi was just about to give a sample for an organization-wide policy manual to her manager for his manager to review. As she was carrying it down the hall, she bumped into a coworker who was carrying a cup of coffee. The coffee spilled on the manual, leaving a big brown stain on the stark white cover. Panicked, Naomi ran downstairs to the graphic designer who had created the cover and asked for help. Naomi had been very opinionated and demanding during the design process, yet the designer helped her begrudgingly. He finished the work just in time, making Naomi feel as uncomfortable as she had made him feel the first time around.

TAKING THE INITIATIVE

Being proactive simply means thinking and planning ahead. It's the opposite of reactive, which means addressing issues as they happen. Of course, it's not always possible to be proactive all of the time. But there are many ways you can take the initiative to prevent problems before they arise. This will save you and your manager valuable time and effort, and you'll be recognized as someone who can get things done the right way. Elaine, Ben, Kevin, Dina, Reid, and Naomi could have benefited from the smart moves that follow.

Smart Move #164: Follow Your Instincts

An important, but often overlooked strategy for being proactive is to pay attention to your instincts. Like Elaine, if you have a strong sense that something isn't quite right, then it probably isn't. Paranoia aside, check out the reality of the situation and then prevent it from getting any worse. For example, you may notice that your relationship with a coworker seems subtly strained, but you can't put your finger on the source of the problem. The proactive response is to address it with your colleague before it becomes a serious problem. Maybe you have a nagging feeling that the direction you're heading in on a particular project may not be the best one. Rather than dismissing the feeling, go with it. And check with your manager to see if there's something you're missing. Your instincts are powerful, because they are based on your cumulative life experience. Some unconscious part of you often realizes that something is amiss even before your conscious mind can process what it is.

Smart Move #165: Get Organized

Depending on your memory like Ben did, won't cut it. But there are many reliable ways to keep your time and clutter in order. For instance, you can easily manage your time by using formal planners, wall calendars, and electronic organizers. You can organize your desk by making files. Just make sure that your approach fits with your personality style. Forcing yourself to use a system that isn't comfortable for you will only result in more chaos. Check out what others around you do to keep themselves organized. Consider taking a workshop—in-house through the training department, or at a local college or alternative learning center. Getting organized will impress your manager and also prevent you from burning out from the stress that being disorganized creates (see chapter 1).

Smart Move #166: Prevent Gaps in Staff Coverage

You may get so focused on organizing your life or excited about an upcoming vacation, like Kevin, that you don't consult with others before you plan time away. But if your time out of the office coincides with others' time away, you may leave your department without adequate coverage. Discuss your plans with your manager and colleagues before you firm them up. This is especially important during busy work seasons and major holidays. That way everyone can work out a mutually acceptable master plan. Also realize that you may have to compromise.

Smart Move #167: Clarify Fuzzy Information

In the course of a busy day, so much information gets exchanged that sometimes things aren't as clear as they should be. For example, Dina and her manager didn't have the same understanding of the word soon when discussing the deadline. Another confusing scenario may involve a memo from your manager about a department meeting next Wednesday. If you receive it on Tuesday, you might be unsure whether the meeting is the following day or the following week. Rather than guessing, just ask your manager. Many people just assume what an ambiguous comment or written directive means and end up doing the wrong thing. It's so much easier to take the extra minute to clarify what's up before it slips your mind.

Smart Move #168: Send Vital Correspondence In Multiple Ways

It's a very good idea to use a backup method when you are sending information close to a deadline. Reid assumed that he could count on faxing . If Reid had used a back-up method, he would have been fine. Or maybe you're finishing an important document for a manager who is out of town, and she wants to review it for a big client meeting. Typically, you would send an e-mail with an attached file to your manager when she's away. But what if she doesn't have access to a printer? In this case, it's a good idea to send it by fax (if it's not too confidential) or by overnight mail (if you have the time to spare) as a back-up method. That way, if anything goes wrong with the e-mail, your manager will get the document another way.

Smart Move #169: Identify Project VIPs

When you begin a project, find out who the key, related people are right away. Internal VIPs aren't necessarily the individuals who hold the highest titles or the longest tenure with the organization. They're the ones who have the most clout with the project, and can either make your project a living hell or help you enormously. Sometimes this means getting to know, for instance, a high-level administrator's assistant, an in-house graphic designer (like in Naomi's case), a payroll clerk, or the manager of the copy center. Some VIPs change from project to project, while others stay the same. So be careful to treat everyone who you come in contact with, at any level of the organization, with respect. It's not only the right thing to do, but you'll be grateful when you need them to come through for you.

External VIPs include anyone outside of your organization who's involved with your project. For example, you may be organizing a conference or off-site staff development retreat. The guest speakers, outside participants, and vendors (food, transportation, housing, special events, etc.) certainly count as VIPs. You must accommodate all of these people or else you'll have big logistical problems. In addition, an external VIP may complain about you to a higher up in your organization if you don't accommodate her, damaging your reputation. Our smart moves throughout the rest of the topics in this chapter (spotlighting up, hot competencies, standing out, and the bottom line) will give you more strategies for transforming yourself into the most valuable person in your workplace.

Taking Initiative Don'ts

1) Encourage your colleagues to keep their resumes up-to-date, since your intuition tells you that you're all about to lose your jobs.
2) Instigate a radical new dress code.
3) Purge your manager's rolodex (without his consent) to help him get organized.
4) Rearrange your manager's office furniture to give her a boost.
5) Make nonrefundable vacation plans way in advance without checking with your manager.
6) Switch your work hours around to fit with your productivity peaks without asking your manager.
7) Ask many nitpicky questions about everything that comes up before you make a move.
8) Spend a fortune on preventable overnight mail expenses for every project.
9) Bombard your colleagues with duplicate forms of documents for no reason.
10) Kiss up, rather than build a genuine professional relationship with prospective VIPs.

SPOTLIGHTING UP

CHALLENGE: MAKING YOUR MANAGER LOOK GOOD

Cara's boss often got caught in embarrassing situations that the department members should have brought to her attention. Her manager relayed these situations to the group during small staff meetings. And she asked her group to make sure they kept her up to date about important happenings as they occurred. During these meetings, Cara often thought to herself, "That's strange. I knew about that issue, so I figured she did too."

Deciding that these incidents must be flukes, Cara focused on meeting the on-paper requirements for her job. She was always on time in the morning and worked well both independently and as part of a team. Her technical skills were very strong, she maintained a positive attitude, and was pleasant to be around. Cara's manager generally valued the quality of Cara's work. But her manager became increasingly upset at getting blindsided by issues that she believed Cara should have updated her on. Cara couldn't seem to grasp the importance of how to buffer her manager. This weakness in Cara's performance eclipsed her assets and inhibited her career growth.

Preventing Blindsiding

A big part of your job is to make your manager look good by keeping him informed. You can protect your manager in several ways.

Smart Move #170: Know Who Key Players Are and Why They're Key

Know about key players who matter to your manager. Whether you're at a large or small organization, it's in your best interest to determine who the key players are as quickly as possibly. Key players include anyone who wields power, whether they've got a big title or not. Some people who work closely with senior managers are actually very influential in the day-to-day decision-making at your organization. If you're new, read the annual report, get your hands on an organizational flow chart (if one's available), check out the organization's phone directory, and make notes of who's who when others mention people.

Smart Move #171: Get It Right For Your Manager's Manager

Another strategy to prevent your manager from getting blindsided is to make sure you do good work for your manager's superiors and other colleagues. All of this work may be handed in through your manager, and your direct contact with her manager may be limited to elevators, large meetings, or the phone. What motivates and concerns your manager is looking good. Since your manager is ultimately responsible for your work and behavior, making the extra effort to get things right the first time reflects well on your manager. In turn, your manager will be happy with you and will help you get ahead in your career.

Smart Move #172: Speak Up

A third strategy is to share cutting-edge information from the things you learn through your reading, talking with others, daily work, and professional association experiences about your job; happenings in the organization; and the trends in your field with your manager. Don't assume that your manager always becomes aware of hot issues at the same time as you. Even if your manager already knows something you share with him, he'll appreciate that you alerted him to it. This exchange of information will often lead to a discussion of the implications for your department. In this way you'll reinforce your image as a professional and foster a collegial dimension to your relationship with your manager.

For example, somewhere along the line, you'll probably attend some meetings and run into controversy concerning how your department relates to other ones. Unless your manager wants a blow-by-blow account, you don't need to get into things on a micro level. But you should clearly summarize issues that need further guidance from above and/or that someone else is bound to surface to your manager. In these cases, don't just sit on these issues and wait for your manager to come to you for clarification or input. Let her know something is up right away and find out if she agrees that it's a hot issue. If it's really a problem, then determine what, if anything, she wants to do about it.

HOT COMPETENCIES

CHALLENGE: STAYING ON THE CUTTING EDGE

Scott wanted to increase his value at his present organization, as well as make himself a more desirable candidate on the job market. In order to cover his bases, Scott knew he had to stay on the cutting edge of his field. He took internal and external continuing education courses to gain innovative knowledge and job-specific skills. But a lot of Scott's coworkers did the same thing. So, he decided to outdo them by accumulating as many of these courses, and ultimately degrees, as possible. All of this education really helped Scott with the elements that were specific to his job. His manager and coworkers came to recognize him as a highly competent specialist and a valued resource in this respect.

When his organization went through a major restructuring, however, Scott was surprised to discover that his manager had to fight to keep him on board. And, through his outside interviews, Scott learned that his specialized proficiencies were not enough. It turned out that both his current and prospective employers sought employees who had both outstanding specialized and general skills. Scott learned that trends such as globalization and management approaches that emphasized teamwork and employee initiative made general skills requirements. Scott thought that a person was either born with soft skills—like teamwork, leadership, and communication—or that he wasn't. So he hadn't paid much attention to developing them, and it showed.

MASTERING KEY SKILLS

Scott's first mistake was writing off general skills as insignificant, or soft. His second mistake was his assumption that these skills couldn't be learned. It's true that some people seem to have a natural ability for things like communication or teamwork (it's also true that some people have natural gifts for specialized skills). However, while some people may be limited in their abilities to develop even a basic level of certain specialized skills, everyone can develop at least a basic level of general skills.

Smart Move #173: Pay Attention to What You Need

It's best to take the initiative to develop new, relevant general skills before or as soon as you realize you need them. How will you know that you need them? You may find out during a performance review. Or, others may get praised for using these skills and you may realize that they're valuable for you too. Your manager may informally mention to your department or just to you that acquiring a certain skill would be an asset to the department. Sometimes the head of an organization announces a firm-wide initiative to improve certain general skills in all employees.

Smart Move #174: Pick a Way to Develop A New Competency

Once you've identified what skills you need to work on, you'll discover that there are many ways to learn these skills. So it should be relatively easy to make room in your schedule for this commitment. For example, if your oral communication skills are weak, you could take an in-house training course on the subject. If your company doesn't offer in-house training, you can attend a public speaking workshop at a community college or school of continuing education or nonprofit organization. Alternatively, you could purchase a book, audiocassette, or videotape on the topic and study it independently (see the Appendix for references).

Smart Move #175: Keep Your New Competency Fresh

Once you devote your time to really developing a hot competency, it's important to find or create ways to maintain this skill. Take advantage of opportunities on the job, through volunteer experiences, or informally—with friends and family, to practice applying this new skill in real life situations. For example, you could practice public speaking by giving a presentation to a group of summer interns in your workplace. If you already volunteer at a nonprofit organization, you could offer to train a group of new volunteers. You could also use personal gatherings, such as weddings or birthday parties, to practice this skill. Making a toast in front of as few—or as many—people you feel comfortable with is a great way to try it out in a supportive atmosphere.

Smart Move #176: Make a Development Plan

Clearly, the payoffs to developing and maintaining general, hot competencies are that you can save or advance your career by integrating them with your specialized proficiencies. But in order to work on these general, hot competencies, you first need to identify which ones you need to develop, which ones you need to maintain, and how to do it. The following exercise can help you to identify and meet your needs.

Hot Competencies Exercise

Part I: Assessing Your Situation

Directions: Put a check in the Develop column next to each competency that you feel you need to work on at a basic or introductory level. Put a check in the Maintain column next to each competency that you believe you have developed to some extent but need to maintain. In the How column, use the code list on the bottom of the chart to select specific ways that you could either develop or maintain each competency. List as many ways as apply for you.

General, Hot Competency	Develop	Maintain	How
Teamwork			
Critical & Creative Thinking/Problem-Solving			
Leadership			
Risk-Taking			
Trust-Building			
Long-term Vision			
Flexibility			
Written Communication			
Oral Communication			
Time/Stress Management			
Conflict Resolution/Mediation			
Other			

How Code List

IHTC = In-House Training Course   OTJ = On-the-Job Opportunities

OTC = Outside Training Course   VO = Volunteer Opportunities

PC = Private Coach   IO = Informal Opportunities

IS = Independent Study (books, audiocassettes, videotapes, etc.)

Directions: Now, based on your particular situation (time, job requirements, and learning style preference), prioritize these competencies and methods for achieving them in the following chart. Also select specific action steps (e.g., names of courses, coaches, books, or opportunities) you'll take to achieve them and corresponding timetables (e.g., dates of courses, and days/weeks/months for coaching, independent study, or other opportunities). Remember to be realistic so that you can achieve your goals.

Competency	Priority Ranking	How Specifics	Specifics	Timetable
Teamwork				
Critical & Creative Thinking/ Problem-Solving				
Leadership				
Risk-Taking				
Trust-Building				
Long-Term Vision				
Flexibility				
Written Communication				
Oral Communication				
Time Stress Management				
Conflict resolution/Mediation				
Other:				

How Code List

IHTC = In-House Training Course   OTJ = On-the-Job Opportunities

OTC = Outside Training Course   VO = Volunteer Opportunities

PC = Private Coach   IO = Informal Opportunities

IS = Independent Study (books, audiocassettes, videotapes, etc.)

CHALLENGE: PROVING YOUR DISTINCTIVENESS

Mara knew that she needed to do more to make herself stand out from her coworkers in order to get ahead in her career. She had mastered many specialized and general skills. She knew how to apply them to enhance her job performance and make her valuable to her manager. But Mara still felt like there was something more she should be doing. Her organization was highly competitive and filled with smart, competent people. Mara often felt like just another number, and worried that she'd never be able to prove to her manager that she was a unique contributor.

USING SPECIAL SKILLS TO ADD VALUE

Mastering both general and specialized skills is only part of the way you can make yourself indispensable to your employer. What Mara didn't know is that to really make yourself stand out, you need to demonstrate your strongest, most relevant skills as frequently as possible.

Smart Move #177: Assess Your Special Skills

Special Skills Exercise

Directions: Put a check next to any skills below that you believe are your strengths. You don't have to be an expert at any of these, just proficient at them.

Communication Skills

Written Communication
_____ report writing
_____ researching
_____ editing
_____ proofreading
_____ translating
_____ summarizing
_____ creative writing
_____ letter writing
_____ journal or diary writing

Interpersonal Communication
_____ advising
_____ counseling
_____ coaching
_____ motivating
_____ arbitrating
_____ leading
_____ negotiating
_____ conversing
_____ listening
_____ teaching
_____ influencing
_____ public speaking

Creative Skills

_____ illustrating
_____ painting
_____ sculpting
_____ composing music
_____ playing music
_____ singing
_____ photography
_____ interior decorating
_____ coming up with new ideas
_____ acting
_____ landscaping
_____ cooking
_____ entertaining
_____ inventing
_____ trouble-shooting

Management Skills

_____ giving orders/delegating
_____ problem-solving
_____ decision-making
_____ supervising
_____ handling details
_____ following-through
_____ accomplishing
_____ planning strategy
_____ setting schedules
_____ controlling
_____ being assertive
_____ competing
_____ organizing
_____ being a team member

Analytical Skills	**Technical Skills**
_____ assessing needs	_____ word processing/typing
_____ interpreting literature	_____ bookkeeping/accounting
_____ mathematical ability	_____ carpentry
_____ understanding finance	_____ working with tools
_____ investment planning	_____ laboratory skills
_____ statistical analysis	_____ working with machines
_____ investigating	_____ graphic design
	_____ computer use
	_____ auto repair
	_____ physical coordination/ strength

Count how many skills you checked in each category. Place the total for the categories in the following blanks. This will give you an idea of what broad skill categories most of your selected skills fall into.

_____ Written Communication Skills

_____ Interpersonal Communication Skills

_____ Creative Skills

_____ Management Skills

_____ Analytical Skills

_____ Technical Skills

Now look back over the skills you checked and circle the ones that you feel are your strongest abilities. Write them (and any not listed) in the space below, listing as few or as many as you'd like.

_____   _____

_____   _____

_____   _____

Smart Move #178: Select Unique Skills

It's particularly important to focus on special skills that distinguish you from your peers. If you have a flair for facilitating meetings, for example, then offer to take on this leadership role in your projects. Creative problem-solving may be your gift. Take the initiative to share your brainstorming abilities with others. Or, you may be good at using certain kinds of computer software, like specialized graphics programs. Produce (and show others how) enhanced reports and presentation materials. Perhaps you have a special aptitude for foreign languages. Then use this ability to develop relationships or help others communicate better with your colleagues or outside clients whose first language isn't English.

Smart Move #179: Focus on Enjoyable Skills

It's really important to pick skills that are not only unique to you, but also those that you genuinely enjoy using. Implementing this strategy may help you become known and depended on as the meeting facilitator, brainstorming, desktop publishing, or foreign language guru. In turn, by developing a reputation in a specialized niche, you can possibly turn it into a new job. Using the skills above, for example, you could become a trainer, creative director, graphic designer, or translator, respectively. If you don't want to redirect your career in this way, make sure you balance getting noticed for your specialized skills with establishing a history of executing the rest of your responsibilities.

Smart Move #180: Pick Relevant Skills

Now that you've identified your strong skills that are unique and enjoyable, you need to screen them for their relevance. You may be great at and love gardening, but this skill won't add any value to your current job. In order for a skill to help you stand out, it must add value to your organization. You can figure out if a skill fits this criterion in one of two ways. First, it may be something that managers at your organization want someone to be able to do. Second, it may be a related, or seemingly unrelated skill that you find a creative way to contribute to your organization. In the second case, you can come up with a solid connection between a skill and how it can help your organization achieve its goals. For example, you might be an advertising account manager who used your knowledge of rare coins to develop a relationship with a prospective client who also collects them. This connection helps you to land a major campaign for laundry detergent. When you've narrowed down your list of special skills to the one or ones that are unique, enjoyable, and relevant, then you're on your way to standing out.

THE BOTTOM LINE

CHALLENGE: BEING PERCEIVED AS A REVENUE PROTECTOR

Jack worked as a recruiter at a large investment bank. He recognized that his job could make a significant difference in the quality of the workforce at his organization and, in turn, in its ability to generate revenue. Others in the organization valued recruiters for helping them staff their departments. But because of the indirect link between recruiters and income, others didn't perceive recruiters as revenue generators. They lumped recruiters together with the majority of the organization that was scrutinized on a regular basis for their expenditures. Recruiting budgets, department birthday parties, and even types of binder clips were issues. Jack became frustrated with his status as a nonproducer and the unwanted budgetary attention his department got from the higher ups in the organization. He wondered if he should try to become a trader so at least he'd be treated with respect as a revenue generator.

PRODUCING HIGH-QUALITY, COST-EFFECTIVE WORK

Someone should have told Jack's managers that just because your job isn't inherently perceived as revenue generating doesn't mean that you can't be a revenue protector, or someone who works in a visibly cost-effective way. Whatever job you hold in any kind of organization, it's your responsibility to help mind the bottom line. You can be an outstanding performer in every way. But if you don't watch your spending, you won't have a shot at becoming the office MVP.

Smart Move #181: Know How Your Organization Defines Cost-Effective

First, make sure that you understand your particular organizational culture's definition of cost-effective. One organization may consider one practice inappropriately cheap, while another organization considers it to be smart financial management.

In Jack's case, for example, he could save his organization big bucks by significantly reducing or eliminating his dependence on outside agencies to find qualified job applicants for the positions he's seeking to fill. Jack could instead implement an employee referral program to motivate current employees to refer their qualified friends and colleagues to him and the other recruiters. Such a program would reward the employee who made the referral with a financial incentive (less than an outside agency would receive, of course) if the candidate was hired and remained in good standing for a period of, for example, six months.

Another way he could cut recruiting costs would be to host on-site job fairs. These fairs typically are advertised in major newspapers and are all day opportunities for prospective job candidates to visit the organization and interview with a recruiter. This is a particularly cost-effective measure for finding candidates for hard-to-fill positions, such as those in information technology. Technical recruiters at employment agencies charge a premium to place qualified computer programmers and related professionals.

Smart Move #182: Find Small Ways to Save Money

Even if you don't feel like you have the opportunity to save your organization lots of money, you can find small ways to save money that collectively make a difference. For example, you can plan low-budget birthday celebrations for coworkers. Also, proactively seek ways to cut outside vendor expenses by doing more yourself. For instance, do more desktop publishing projects in-house, rather than outsourcing graphic design work. And aggressively shop around for competitive rates on services you must outsource. Sometimes organizations get in the habit of using a vendor for years without ever comparing prices or renegotiating rates. Whenever possible, streamline administrative processes so that you eliminate wasting products like paper and money on people power.

Smart Move #183: Show That You're a Bottom-Liner

A bottom-liner is someone who works in a visibly cost-effective way. In order to ensure that you're perceived as a bottom-liner, let your manager know what you're up to by documenting your actions and quantifying your results whenever possible. Naturally, you don't want to bombard your manager with daily or weekly updates on how much you saved on pens. But mention the big stuff and lump the little stuff together on a periodic basis. By using your accomplishment log (see chapter 3, accomplishment logs section) to keep track of your efforts, you can insert them into project reports, update memos, and performance reviews.

5

Dealing With Change In Your Organization

WORK SMART IQ QUIZ #5

Review each item below and decide if it's a work smart myth or a work smart reality. In the space before each statement, put an "M" if you think it's a myth and an "R" if you think it's a reality. Then check your responses with the correct answers at the end of the quiz.

_____ 1. The more chaotic things get during or after a merger, downsizing, restructuring or other "unnatural disaster" that's out of your control, the more you should try to control the situation.

_____ 2. Minimize your stress during an "unnatural disaster" by talking it out with someone who is supportive and trustworthy.

_____ 3. Vent your frustrations about your manager or organization in a restaurant or on public transportation.

_____ 4. Stressful times are ideal for seeking creative and physical outlets, like a sculpture class or a gym membership.

_____ 5. Ignore rumors during times of radical change in your organization.

_____ 6. Given the rapid pace of change in the world of work, you must pursue further training to enhance your skills or to gain new ones throughout your career.

_____ 7. During "unnatural disasters," you should put your networking on hold until the dust settles and you know who the new or remaining key players will be in your organization.

_____ 8. Transferring internally is a less desirable career move than getting another job outside of your organization.

_____ 9. As long as you handle the emotional, financial, and career move challenges, becoming unemployed can turn out to be more of a golden opportunity than a traumatic experience.

_____ 10. The real key to achieving balance in your life and working smart is to focus on the future.

Answers: (1)-M, (2)-R, (3)-M, (4)-R, (5)-R, (6)-R, (7)-M, (8)-M, (9)-R, (10)-M

UNNATURAL DISASTERS

CHALLENGE: COPING WITH TURBULENT TIMES

Susan had worked at the same company since she graduated from college three years before. At first, she had considered herself lucky to find such a good fit and had looked forward to going to work every morning. Then her company merged with another company and the subsequent restructuring transformed what had been a predictable, energizing workplace into a chaotic one. Most of Susan's former long-term projects were suddenly derailed. The two former organization's cultures were very different, resulting in a lot of tension as the senior managers tried to mesh the two groups of employees. Everyone was worried about losing their jobs or getting relocated. Susan became increasingly unhappy and dreaded going to work.

Susan wasn't sure if it was okay to discuss her concerns at work. Everyone, including her manager, walked around looking distracted and keeping their feelings pretty much to themselves. Guessing which departments might be eliminated was the prime topic of conversation. Susan tried unsuccessfully to cope with the many different rumors circulating hourly. And she was reluctant to approach her manager about her job priorities, because she didn't want to attract negative attention to herself. Ultimately, Susan decided that blending into the crowd was better than making herself a target for possible firing.

MEETING BOTH YOUR NEEDS AND THEIRS

It's really tough to cope with the stress in the workplace caused by mergers, downsizing, and restructuring. As in Susan's situation, projects often will be axed abruptly or put on hold indefinitely. There may be a lot of tension due to clashing cultures. You may lose perks that drew you to the job in the first place (like tuition reimbursement) even if you're in the middle of benefiting from them. Your responsibilities may radically change and you may get assigned a heavier work load. You may have to deal with losing your job, and at the very least you'll face the overwhelming fear of losing it. You may be given the ultimatum to relocate or pack it in. Your manager may be absorbed by her own problems, which will only add to your feelings of isolation. However, there are things you can do to help you deal with these situations.

Smart Move #184: Don't Try to Control the Uncontrollable

It's natural to want more control in a situation spinning out of it. But, in reality, you can't single-handedly impose order on things. The only thing you can do is try to control your reactions to the chaos by going with the flow. Know that the situation is and will be messy for a while. It's a tough, stressful situation. And it's not your imagination, even if others' are slow to acknowledge how difficult things get. Try to simplify your work and personal lives by making them as stress-free as possible to offset the stress going on around you.

Smart Move #185: Talk It Out With the Right People

One way to minimize your stress is to discuss it with others going through the same thing. If your manager is receptive or if formal groups are organized at work to discuss these issues, then you can work through your experience there. More commonly, though, you'll need to look for outside support. Work-sponsored employee assistance programs, your mentor, your significant other, and friends are all valuable candidates for your support system. Just be careful not to overload those in your personal life.

Also, when you're under stress at work, it's tempting to tear into your organization when riding on public transportation or in restaurants and other public places. Be extra discreet under these circumstances, since you never know who may overhear you. Someone from another organization, where you may want to interview, may also overhear you and form a negative impression of you as a bitter, disloyal employee.

Smart Move #186: Seek Creative and Physical Outlets

Stressful times are ideal for seeking creative and/or physical outlets. These activities both help you to relieve stress and promote your personal growth. It's also an ideal way to meet others with common interests who aren't involved in the ebb and flow of your work life.

Smart Move #187: Ignore the Rumors

While you're getting away from it all, you'll hopefully gain the perspective that there's no objective "truth" to be known about what's really going on at work. Under these circumstances, it may change from moment to moment. So it's not worth your energy to get caught up in following the trail of rumors and overreacting to them. Most people won't really know what's up, just those at the top. Since you'll know when the senior managers want you to know, you may as well just wait it out.

Smart Move #188: Prove Yourself By Maintaining a Professional Demeanor

It's understandable to feel confused about how to do a good job in these situations. Getting clear on priorities, setting limits with your manager about your work load, dealing with culture clashes, and trying to be a team player while watching out for your best interests may seem like impossible tasks.

Ironically, much of your job during and in the wake of unnatural disasters is actually managing your stress level so that you can be as productive as possible. Senior managers will be watching for people who can handle themselves well under pressure and maintain their professionalism. So do your best to be choosey about challenging your manager. Don't question priorities incessantly, especially if you keep getting ambiguous responses. As for clashing cultures, don't let yourself get caught up in the "us" versus "them" mentality. Be a team player and still watch out for your own interests by looking for ways to keep learning and growing professionally while the disaster takes its course.

Our smart moves throughout the rest of the topics in this chapter—survival training, networking for options, transferring ins and outs, unemployment, and balancing your life—lead you through other ways to cope with change in your organization.

SURVIVAL TRAINING

Challenge: Stabilizing Your Current Job or Preparing to Move On

Zach, Hilary, Jeremy, and Molly worked at a company that was downsizing. They all wanted to keep their options open for stabilizing their current jobs or moving on to new ones. Training seemed like a logical step for them all, but they had different concerns related to pursuing it. Zach was concerned about taking time away from his busy job for classes to strengthen his skill sets. Hilary's internal training options were frozen for the time being, and she was unsure about other possibilities. Jeremy was skeptical of the value of training in both his employer's and his own eyes. Molly was so stressed and overextended from dealing with her career on the job that she didn't want to deal with more exposure to the same topic during her own time.

CONTINUING YOUR EDUCATION

For every reason you can come up with to avoid taking classes—like Zach's, Hilary's, Jeremy's, and Molly's—there's a better reason to do it. Workers at every stage of their careers should seek further training to enhance their skills or gain new ones. More than ever, a critical aspect of working smart is obtaining specialized training to keep your skills current. Given the rapid pace of change in the work world, you must continue your education to keep up with the latest developments.

Smart Move #189: Keep the Time Investment in Perspective

What Zach didn't realize was that, even if he's putting in long hours, he can't develop his career on the job all of the time. So he may as well have spent some of his time doing something outside of work to promote his career development.

Smart Move #190: Explore Outside Training Options

Like Hilary, you may need to explore outside options for getting training. While in-house training classes can be accessible, targeted ways to get or polish your skills, they're only one of a number of options. You can work with a reference librarian or information specialist at your local public library or college's career services office library. You can also ask professors, friends, parents' friends, colleagues, and contacts in your field of interest for their recommendations. Also, use the telephone book, as well as the *Encyclopedia of Associations* in the library to compile a working list of schools and other organizations that may offer courses in your area of interest. Once you have a working list of options, contact the institutions directly and ask them to send you their course catalog and any specific information on your program of interest. For some ideas on the kinds of institutions that offer continuing education courses, see the Continuing Ed Criteria and Options Worksheet at the end of this section.

Smart Move #191: Use Training to Get an Edge

Jeremy was uncertain about the value of training. He liked learning on the job and had done just fine to this point in his career. Everyone, however, can benefit from gaining additional knowledge and skills from other sources than on the job. What you learn from other people—both teachers and students—will enable you to bring a new point of view to your current position and become a stronger candidate for a new job.

Smart Move #192: Take the Path of Least Resistance

Molly assumed that because she was stressed from her job that training would only compound her tension. However, this can prove to be untrue, depending on the kinds of classes, the hidden perks, and how related they are to your current job. Many continuing education options have low pressure requirements. For example, you can take a class that does not require you to do homework. Or, you can take a class not-for-credit. Many classes are flexible for working adults; they may be condensed into all-day weekend workshops or one-hour evening commitments. Be sure to check out your education options thoroughly: Teaching styles vary from lectures to interactive experiences. Prices range from inexpensive to expensive. Classes are often held in locations that are convenient to your workplace or home. And increasing numbers of classes and even graduate programs are offered through distance learning (which means you can do most or all of the classes and required work via your computer and/or mail correspondence with a sponsoring institution).

Smart Move #193: Reignite, Reconnect With, and Review Your Passions

Under the right conditions, you may discover that taking classes may be a fun way to reignite your passion for your field. Continuing your education is a great way to network with others and to utilize career services professionals who are affiliated with the programs. Don't feel like you must take classes that are directly related to your current position. You might want to test new areas of interest to help you begin to make a career or job transition.

Smart Move #194: Figure Out What You Need and Where to Get It

SURVIVAL TRAINING EXERCISE

Directions: Put a check next to any criteria that you have for continuing your education. Then put a check next to any options that seem like viable places to pursue education opportunities or places that you'd at least like to explore as possible options.

CRITERIA

OPTIONS

___ Minimal or no homework

_____ Graduate schools

___ Credit only

_____ Technical training schools

___ Non-credit option	___ Professional associations
___ Evening classes	___ Community colleges
___ Weekend classes	___ Community centers
___ Primarily interactive	___ Alternative learning centers
___ Primarily lectures	___ Continuing education programs through universities
___ Inexpensive	___ Town-sponsored adult schools
___ Close to work	___ Privately-run workshops
___ Close to home	___ Institutes
___ Distance learning	___ Internet classes (through individuals or institutions)
___ Other:	___ Other:
___ Other:	___ Other:

NETWORKING FOR OPTIONS

CHALLENGE: MAXIMIZING YOUR OPPORTUNITIES

Everyone Ian trusted—his mentor, friends, parents, and girl-friend—advised him to get busy networking since his organization and industry were both going through a period of rapid change. They all told Ian to assert himself quickly, so that he didn't get stuck without active job connections in case his position got eliminated.

Ian knew that they were probably right. But he kept making excuses as to why he couldn't network right then. Ian told his mentor he felt so stressed out that he was sure he'd come across to potential employers as a desperate rather than as a self-confident, strong candidate. Ian informed his friends that he was hesitant to network because all of the people in his field were under stress. He didn't feel comfortable bothering them and was convinced that everyone was too busy watching out for themselves. Ian explained to his parents that he didn't even know who to contact, because he was unsure who the key players would be when all the shakeups were over. And Ian shared with his girlfriend his desire to focus on his current job and block out what was going on in order to conserve energy and stay calm.

Generating Choices Through Your Contacts

When you're dealing with industry-driven change in your organization, like Ian, you may not feel like networking with others who are also tense from going through the same kind of change. Although it may seem paradoxical, this is a prime time to draw upon contacts. It's normal to feel shaky, so you may have to fake confidence until you get past the jitters.

Smart Move #195: Polish Your Soundbyte Before You Connect

You can calm your nerves by preparing for contacting members of your network. Before you speak with them, make sure you prepare your *soundbyte*. That is, be able to articulate what you're seeking specifically; what you have to offer; and recent, concrete examples of your accomplishments. Review your accomplishment log to help you remember examples (see the accomplishment logs section in chapter 3).

Smart Move #196: Take Advantage of the Chance to Swap Leads

If your industry as a whole is undergoing change realize that everyone is networking. This means that you can help each other out. Be judicious about who to trust with your plans and leads, however, since there will be a strong competitive spirit pervading the networking atmosphere.

Smart Move #197: Network with Targeted Contacts

As for being unsure about who the key players will be in your organization or field after all of the dust settles, don't paralyze yourself because of something that's out of your control. Trust your instincts and the signs. Chances are, those who've been respected because of their skills and integrity will stay at the top of your organization or another reputable one. You should both maintain established key contacts as well as scout out new ones.

Remember to network with people who you'd potentially want to work for or with. Don't just scramble to get as many hot contacts as possible: If you don't like their values or personality style, there's no point in forging a possible future with them. Unless these situations are very short term, you'll be miserable working in poor-fit situations just for the sake of it. So target high-*quality* as well as a *quantity* of contacts.

Smart Move #198: Initiate Contact and Maintain Momentum

Above all, resist the urge to bury your head in the sand. You may think you're conserving energy, but you're just avoiding the inevitable. Through good networking you'll build a safety net and give yourself a chance to explore other opportunities. After all, no one can offer you a job if they don't know you're receptive to it. Keep yourself fresh in others' minds over time, and they'll present opportunities to you more readily. If you take a proactive approach instead of a reactive one, you'll be less pressured when you've lost your job or quit out of frustration.

Smart Move #199: Track Your Networking

Now that you've realized the importance of networking you'll need to track your process. It's easy to forget who you connected with, when, or the next steps you need to take when you keep it all in your head. Use the sample log that follows to record your contacts. Keep this in your home computer if you have one, or else make a bunch of blank forms and fill them in as you go, keeping them together in a file at home.

Sample Networking Log

Name of Contact:

Referred by:

By Title:

Address:

Phone:

Fax:

E-Mail:

Nature of Contact:

Date:

Follow-up & Date:

TRANSFERRING INS AND OUTS

CHALLENGE: MAKING A MOVE

Dianna was tired of dealing with the stress of all the changes going on at work. She was also questioning her career path in general. When Dianna expressed a desire to make a fresh start at another company, her mentor encouraged her to first explore options for transferring within her current organization. Dianna hadn't even seriously considered this option, as she was fantasizing about a clean break.

Dianna realized that she didn't even know the fundamentals of the transferring process, including when she was eligible to apply for another position, how she could find out about positions, or how to apply for them. Dianna's mentor informed her about advantages like using a transfer to make a lateral move into another field, rather than doing the standard search for a higher-level position within her present field. Dianna further realized that she had let her concerns about the politics of handling the process with her manager stop her from trying. In the end, Dianna's mentor helped her see that she'd dismissed the transferring option based on incomplete information.

MOBILIZING INTERNALLY

When you're entertaining the idea of a job move, don't overlook the option of transferring internally in your organization. Unless you have a strong reason for wanting to completely leave, this can be a solid career move. Many organizations like to promote and move employees around from within. It helps their retention rates and saves them money that they've invested in training good employees. Also, good employees who've been exposed to the way an organization does things and have developed strong internal relationships are valuable people to cross-train. They're already up to speed to some extent and can bring this knowledge—as well as fresh perspectives from another area—into a new department.

Smart Move #200: Find Out How the Process Works

Before you make any rash decisions, get the facts on transferring policies and procedures at your organization. They should be listed in your employee policy manual, circulated by memo, posted in the employment division, or available in some other, easily and confidentially accessible format. Your human resources department may be able to point you in the right direction.

Timing, for example, is critical. You need to determine if you're eligible to apply for a new position. In many companies, for example, you need to have been employed for a year and have had a satisfactory performance review before you can apply for a transfer. Sometimes there's no formal time-related policy, and such requests are reviewed on a case-by-case basis. However, since most companies consider you to be on probation for the first three to six months, it's not a smart move on your part to try to transfer before you've been there for at least six months.

As a newcomer, remember the advice we gave you in chapter 2, transitions section: You're still learning the ropes and getting to scout out opportunities within your current job. So give yourself a chance to make your position work, prove yourself, and get to know what's out there before you attempt to jump to another position. Your organization will think that you're able to make an informed choice about what's a win-win for both of you if you pay your dues first.

Smart Move #201: Keep Checking Out Available Positions

Once you've got the scoop on how the transferring process works, check out the pool of available positions. Keep in mind that they may vary widely, depending on seasonal needs, happenings in the organization (like budget freezes), and other organization-specific factors. So you may want to review the offerings regularly over a period of time before you decide that there's nothing there for you. Some organizations keep job posting books and/or bulletin boards, job hotlines, and electronic postings on the internal computer network and/or their Web site. Also, the internal networking contacts you've made (see the connections section in chapter 3) can give you the scoop about any prospective openings.

Smart Move #202: Explore Relocation

When you're considering transferring, relocation is another potential benefit and option. Not all transfers within an organization mean merely moving to a new floor in your building. You may have the opportunity to move to a different part of town, or even to a new city, state, or country. In any case, you'll go through a process similar to an external job search in terms of interviewing, evaluating whether it's right for you, and negotiating an offer. Your advantage, of course, is that you're an insider and know a lot about the organization and possibly even the interviewer(s).

Smart Move #203: Consider an Other-Than-Up Move

If you're seeking to make a career shift or want to take a less demanding position for lifestyle reasons, you may need to make a lateral or step-down move. Sometimes it's easier to do this by staying inside of your organization, rather than having to justify your desires to a prospective employer. And if you ultimately want to leave your organization, you can make a short-term inside move and then use it to leverage your chances for an outside position a little down the road. It's a good idea to keep both your short-and long-term goals in mind at all times.

Smart Move #204: Only Tell Others When Necessary

Worrying about potential embarrassment or retribution if you don't get the transfer you apply for is understandable. There's no need to tell your colleagues unless you accept a transfer. It may be tempting to talk about your intentions, but it could end up hurting you. A peer could tell your manager what you're up to before you do. Or your colleague may be applying for the same transfer, which will create a competitive tension between you.

As for your manager, the best way to handle this is to only tell her when and if you have to. For example, if your organization has an internal mobility program, then you'll probably go through a human resources coordinator to express interest in the position. They'll evaluate your fit, present you as a candidate to the hiring manager, and see if they can arrange an interview for you to meet with the manager. At this point in the process, you'll probably need to inform your manager of what's up. Then you'll pursue the position and see what happens. If you don't get to the interview stage of the process, there's no need for you to tell your manager that you've applied for another position.

This scenario may vary from organization to organization, however. For instance, if you work at a very small or tightly knit organization, it's not the best move for you or another manager to directly discuss hiring you for another position behind your manager's back. You can certainly build a relationship with another manager over time, however. And they, in turn, can approach your manager about taking you on (so there's always a politically correct way to handle such situations). Just remember to pay attention to how things are done at your organization (see the culture section in chapter 2).

Smart Move #205: Carry On With Business As Usual

Regardless of the exact nature of the application process and your company's culture, it's important that you continue with business as usual during and after you apply. Continue to actively demonstrate your commitment to, and enthusiasm for, your current position. That way, whether you take the new job or not, you minimize your risk of jeopardizing your good standing with your present manager.

UNEMPLOYMENT

CHALLENGE: HANDLING UNEMPLOYMENT

Charlie was let go for performance reasons. Isabella got laid off during a downsizing. Daryl lost his job when his company went bankrupt. Collectively, they experienced a wide range of emotions: They felt shocked, angry, frustrated, rejected, betrayed, sad, embarrassed, hopeless, and even relieved. In addition, they all had financial concerns about what compensation they were entitled to as well as how to stabilize themselves for the short term. They also all wanted to know about their job and career options.

Moving Your Career Forward

Depending on the circumstances and your state of mind, becoming unemployed can be one of the most traumatic experiences or one of the biggest gifts in your life. For example, if you're let go like Charlie and you didn't want to be, you're obviously not going to be happy about it. But if you're laid off during a downsizing like Isabella, you may end up getting a decent financial package and possibly even free outplacement counseling (a type of career and job placement counseling). Sometimes employees can choose to take such a package and leave willingly. This is especially true if they're thinking about an organization or career change anyway. In Daryl's situation, it could be a stresser *or* a blessing. A lot depends on how suddenly you lose your job and what the financial implications are for you.

In the smart moves that follow we'll discuss the three main things you have to deal with when you become unemployed: your emotional reactions, your financial considerations, and your next career move.

Smart Move # 206: Manage Your Emotions

Being unemployed can feel like a never-ending roller coaster ride. One minute you're climbing to the top of a steep hill, brimming with hope and anticipation. The next minute you're being propelled down into a valley, screaming in terror. You may even go upside down and around in loops for a while before the ride comes to a stop. But, like a roller coaster ride, know that you're unemployment, and the range of emotions that come from being unemployed, *will* come to an end. One way to deal with your emotional reactions to losing your job is to become aware of the way you think about being rejected. For example, you may feel worthless and think things like, "There's no point in searching for another job because I'm not competent enough to keep one." Interrupt such thoughts and edit them into more positive ones, such as "It's only one job. I've been perceived as capable and valuable in the past and will be again." Or you may feel embarrassed and think things like, " I just want to stay at home and hide until I straighten my life out." Instead, think, "It's not shameful to be rejected. I will surround myself with those I trust who are supportive of my endeavors." Or, you may feel angry and think things like, "That organization is full of a bunch of crazy jerks!" Instead, think, "I can get another job that is an even better fit with who I am and what I want."

Another way to cope with the rejection of unemployment is to review your past successes. This is an excellent time to go find your accomplishment log and read through it (see chapter 3, accomplishment logs section). Focusing on your achievements over time can inspire and ground you. You will remember what you love to do and what you do well. This can help you find a direction as you regroup to move ahead in your career.

Taking care of your yourself in every way is especially important when you're unemployed. It may not be your first priority, but get back to the basics in your life—eating well, sleeping enough, exercising, and socializing, among other things. Do some fun, inexpensive things that make you really happy. Take a nature walk or watch your favorite funny movie. The better you treat yourself, the more energy and clarity you'll have to figure out what to do next in your career.

Losing your job is an isolating experience. You'll need to create a support system of people who you can turn to when you're feeling really down. This support system can be as big or as small as you wish. It's a good idea, though, to have more than one supporter in order to benefit from others' varied experiences and to avoid putting too much pressure on any one relationship. Also, remember to select others who you can also support at some point in their careers. That way you'll feel more at ease about leaning on them now. (See the transition resources section in chapter 8.)

Smart Move # 207: Develop a Financial Plan

Naturally, money is one of the first things that comes to mind when you lose your job. You'll need to take a systematic approach to your finances: First, define the problem. Ask yourself: What is my current financial situation? Review your personal resources as well as any compensation that is owed to you, such as severance pay or unemployment.

Second, determine how much money you really need to live for different, specific periods of time until you find another job (e.g., 3 months, 6 months, 1 year, etc.). Remember to consider medical benefits, any outstanding debts that you are repaying such as student loans or car payments, and money for emergencies. Be conservative in your estimates. Use canceled checks and review your monthly budget if you have one to determine what your real costs are, not what you wish they would be.

Third, calculate the difference between your financial resources and your financial needs. Again, be honest. This is a good time to cut back on luxuries such as eating out. (But it's *not* the time to decide to eat one meal a day or live with no heat in the middle of the winter.)

Fourth, review your options. Ask yourself: What are my choices? Be creative and brainstorm every possible way that you can close the gap between your resources and needs. For example, your list may include: borrow money from my parents, run up x dollars on my credit card, dip into my savings account, and get a part-time job.

Fifth, consider the consequences of each option. Ask yourself: What would the likely outcome be, for instance, if I borrowed money from my parents? Think about any previous times you've borrowed money from your folks. Were they sympathetic and generous or were they indifferent and stingy? Did they help you out with a smile and reassuring word, or did they lecture you on the value of money and hard work?

Sixth, factor in your financial comfort level. Ask yourself: If I do x, can I live with the likely outcome? You may be fairly certain that following a certain course of action will resolve the problem. But you may not feel comfortable taking that action or with the consequences of it.

Seventh, get some help if you need it. Ask yourself: Do I need some advice from a more experienced professional? A knowledgeable friend or parent can sometimes be very helpful when you're overwhelmed by financial stress. They may make suggestions to you about managing your money that you hadn't thought of, and that may take the pressure off for a while.

Eighth, make a new budget and financial plan. Then stick to it. Once you know exactly what your cost of living is and how you're going to deal with it, you can focus on getting your career back on track. Otherwise, your financial woes will preoccupy you and potentially multiply if you don't get them under control.

Smart Move #208: Consider Making a Career Move

Losing your job is a lot like moving, because you sort through old stuff. Once you determine if each item fits with your current lifestyle, you then can decide whether to save it, toss it, or reuse it in a new way. Concerning your career, you can review each aspect of your last job—your work hours, dress code, manager's style, nature of your responsibilities, etc. Then you can decide which aspects you want to keep or change and which ones you want to dump in your next job.

Once you've reflected on the good and bad parts of your former position, you can focus your energy on your next move. You may want to look for the same job in another company, or you may want to look for an entirely new job. You may want to work part-time instead of full-time. Alternatively, you may decide to go back to school or take some time to travel or volunteer. Or, you may want to combine some of these options. For example, you can take a part-time job, a volunteer position in your field of interest, and a related continuing education class to make the transition into a new or slightly different field.

Whatever you decide to do, make sure that you give yourself enough structure in your newly unemployed life. Otherwise, it's easy to fall into a lazy routine of sleeping late and letting the day slip by without working on your next career move. If you're doing a job or volunteer position search, get up and dress every day just as you would if you were going to work. Set up a makeshift desk if you don't already have one. Whether you're exploring career options, searching for a job or volunteer position, or researching school programs or travel opportunities, organize your day accordingly. For example, you may do library research in the morning, and make phone calls and write letters to network or request materials in the afternoon. Consider your job during this interim time as being a career move explorer and maker.

Of course, you may be completely confused about what to do next. In this case, see chapter 6 to decide if you should make a career change and, if you do, check out chapter 7 to learn about how to find the best new career for you.

BALANCING YOUR LIFE

CHALLENGE: HAVING IT ALL

Josh had juggled a full schedule of sports, advanced classes, and a serious relationship in college. So he expected it to be relatively easy to maintain this kind of lifestyle in his first job after college. But substituting a professional job for schoolwork threw him off balance. He wasn't used to the rigid structure and constant demands that his job required. As a result, Josh's girlfriend complained that he was too preoccupied with thoughts of work. And he showed up at soccer games too tired to play well or even have fun.

Chloe loved dedicating most of her energy and time to her job when she was a recent grad. But a few years later, as a young professional and new mother, she wasn't happy with her work-heavy lifestyle anymore. Chloe knew that her priorities had changed, but she didn't give herself a chance to even think through what was different than before. Since she didn't know what she wanted, Chloe couldn't adjust her work life accordingly and continued to be unhappy for almost a year. Finally, Chloe took a vacation and slowed down enough for a few days to realize that she wanted more time with her son, to pursue her former hobby of photography, and to do yoga and a workout a few times a week.

Noah often daydreamed for several hours a day. These visions alternated between fantasies about how he would make it big in his field and fantasies about how he would be the best husband in the world. At night though, Noah had recurring nightmares about repeating his past failed attempts to succeed in balancing his work and his relationship. Noah therefore spent most of his time thinking about his past or his future.

Getting It Together

There is a lot of media hype about how easy it is to create a balanced life. But recent grads or young professional, like Josh, Chloe, and Noah know that it's one thing to *value* a sane, fulfilling life, but another thing to actually live that life. During this paying-your-dues stage of your career, you're exploring your work options and figuring out the rules of working smart. Work probably takes up a significant portion of your time and energy. And even when you're not working, you may think and talk about it. Although it's tough to find a comfortable balance between your personal and work lives, it's possible. The smart moves below are a few guidelines to keep in mind.

Smart Move #209: Have It All Over Time

Having it all is possible. But not all at once. It's great to have big, ambitious goals for your work and personal lives like Josh. Just remember that achieving these types of goals requires a lot of time, energy, and persistence. Often, it's not humanly possible to reach more than one of these goals at once. For instance, training successfully to climb Mt. Everest, holding down a 60-hour a week job, and taking care of a new baby would be pushing it for anyone. In order to give yourself the best chance of achieving your goals, be realistic. Take the path of least resistance by striving for what you want under the best conditions possible. Otherwise, you're setting yourself up for failure as surely as if you were to start that Mt. Everest climb during a blizzard. (To learn more about how your work and personal life are highly interdependent and how problems in your personal life can make you unhappy at work and vice-versa, see the avoiding the cop-out section in chapter 6.)

Smart Move #210: Know That Your Priorities Will Change

What's important to you about your work life will likely be very different at different points in your career. But this isn't just, for example, because you may decide you'd prefer to wear jeans rather than a suit. Many people, such as Chloe, find that changes in their personal life profoundly affect their work life needs as well. For example, you may want to telecommute—work from home—a couple of days a week, or move so that you can spend more time with your family. Or, you may decide that you've spent too many years working long hours and want more time to pursue a social life or hobbies. Maybe you've let your physical health deteriorate because you've over-focused on work responsibilities and been under too much stress.

Whatever the reason, when you want to alter the balance of your work and personal lives, it usually requires a tradeoff. For instance, if you work out a partial telecommuting arrangement, you may have to cram more meetings in on the days that you're in the office. If you want to make room for a social life or hobbies, you may have to forgo some work-related activities like playing on the company softball team or attending every cocktail party. In turn, you may lose some political clout. If you want to reduce your stress and nurture your health, you may need to give up some of your responsibilities or change jobs. Change, even for the better, is often scary and not easy to make for many people. But the upside to these compromises is that you can achieve a more balanced life.

Smart Move #211: Close the Gaps

Periodically in your life, take a moment to step back from your daily routine and reflect on what's going on. Consider how you're spending your time and what you ideally want to be doing. If there are any unaccounted-for gaps between your real and ideal lives, then make a plan for how to address closing these gaps. Again, keep in mind that this plan may involve many longer-term steps, but that's okay. The most important thing is that you're consciously navigating your life path. Otherwise, it's easy to, like Chloe, get caught up in the daily bustle of your everyday existence and let time slip away while you're slowly becoming off balance and frustrated.

Smart Move #212: Live in the Present

Many people, like Noah, waste precious time dwelling on past failures to balance their lives, fearing future failures, or scheming for future moments of glory. They daydream or feel guilty about the part of their lives they're not attending to at the time—their personal lives while at work, and work during their off–hours.

The real key to achieving balance and working smart is to devote less attention to the past and the future than to the present. After all, the here and now is the only thing you have to work with directly. Pause to celebrate what you enjoy and your present accomplishments in each aspect of your life, no matter how small or insignificant they may seem at the moment.

III

How to Change Careers

CHAPTER 6

Deciding if You Should Make a Career Change

WORK SMART IQ QUIZ #6

Review each item below and decide if it's a work smart myth or a work smart reality. In the space before each statement, put an M if you think it's a myth and an R if you think it's a reality. Then check your responses with the correct answers at the end of the quiz.

_____ **1.** The definition of a career change is switching from one field to a completely different one.

_____ **2.** It's helpful to keep a record of your thoughts about the problems with your current career and what type of change you'd like to make.

_____ **3.** When you're not happy or not doing well on your job, or don't seem to be getting anywhere in your career in general, then it's definitely time for a career change.

_____ **4.** Your personal and professional lives are separate entities, so how happy you are in one doesn't affect the other.

_____ 5. Even if you don't end up following it, get input from family, friends, professional colleagues, or career development experts before making a career change decision.

_____ 6. If you make a career change as a young professional, you'll ruin your reputation and your chance for success.

_____ 7. The average person these days changes careers at least three times in a lifetime.

_____ 8. Most recent grads and young professionals today are more concerned about liking their job than with their level of job security.

_____ 9. Decreasing numbers of recent grads are interested in helping professions, like teaching, and fewer are involved in community service.

_____ 10. If you leave a job before you've been there for a year, you'll be labeled as a "job hopper."

Answers: (1)-M, (2)-R, (3)-M, (4)-M, (5)-R, (6)-M, (7)-R, (8)-R, (9)-M, (10)-M

THE ROOTS OF DISSATISFACTION

CHALLENGE: FIGURING OUT EXACTLY WHAT'S WRONG WITH YOUR CAREER

Veronica had worked in public relations for five years since graduating college—a career she had kind of stumbled into after interning in a small public relations firm during her senior year. After graduation, she was hired to be an assistant in that same firm. She stayed there for two years, then moved to a medium-sized firm for another two years, where she began as an assistant and later moved up to an account coordinator position. Veronica was then offered the job she had been aiming for all along: an account coordinator at a very large firm—one of the top agencies in the public relations industry, with major accounts, and offices worldwide. Veronica accepted the job and expected to be thoroughly satisfied with her career. But she wasn't. After almost a year there, she found herself hating her job and growing increasingly disenchanted with public relations in general. She wanted to resign, but wasn't sure if she should get another public relations job or should change career fields entirely. Veronica desperately wanted to make a move but didn't know what kind of move made sense.

Jamie faced a similar dilemma. He was just two years out of college and already questioning the career path he was on. All through college he had thought he wanted to head toward a career in sales. Sales seemed to be where the money was, and he knew he wanted to make big bucks. So, he was thrilled when he got his first postgraduate job as a sales rep for a major software company. Jamie had always been technically inclined and had a lot of experience with computers, so he really understood the products he would be selling. He had also worked in retail sales positions during summers off from college, so he had a basic understanding of what sales and customer service was all about. Soon after he started his job with the software company, however, Jamie began to be disillusioned with sales. He had a lot of conflicts with his boss, who was always on his back to make more cold calls and close more deals. Jamie also found that he enjoyed reading his products' technical manuals and hanging around the product development team (i.e., the programmers and technicians) more than he enjoyed calling on customers. He started dreading going to work every day and knew that he needed to make some kind of change. Jamie just wasn't sure if he should find a sales job with a different company or should get out of sales entirely.

DEFINE THE KIND OF CHANGE YOU NEED

The confusion that Veronica and Jamie experienced is typical of people contemplating a career change. If you find that you've tried to make your job work or your career path feel right (by using the techniques suggested in parts one and two of this book), but you're still unhappy, then a career change might be just what you need. It's important, though, to think carefully before jumping into a new career field. A first step in doing so is to identify the roots of your dissatisfaction. Are you thinking of leaving your career field entirely because you hate your boss, when all you really need is a transfer to a new department or the same type of job in a new company? Do you dislike your job responsibilities and the career track that this job has put you on? In that case, a true career change might be in order. In order to know what kind of change you're looking for, and even to know if any move at all is justified, you need to figure out exactly what the problem is. The smart moves that follow will help you do just that.

Smart Move #213: The "What's Bugging You" Quiz

What's Bugging You—

A Quiz to Determine If a Career Change is the Answer

Directions: Read each of the following statements and circle Y for yes or N for no to reflect whether each statement describes your situation, feelings, or thoughts about your job and career at this time. (Note that "job" refers to your current employment, while "career field" refers to your overall occupation, e.g., public relations, finance, computer programming, physical therapy, law, etc.)

1. I dislike, or am bored with, the projects or responsibilities I currently have.

    Y   N

2. My skills and abilities are not being used to their full extent.

    Y   N

3. I am required to do things on my job that don't come naturally to me.

    Y   N

4. I do not get the recognition I deserve when I do my job well.

    Y   N

5. I am unhappy with my work schedule.

    Y   N

6. I don't like my boss.
   Y   N

7. I don't get along with one or more of my coworkers.
   Y   N

8. My physical work space is uncomfortable or not my style.
   Y   N

9. I have ethical conflicts with the organization that employs me.
   Y   N

10. I dislike the management style of my organization.
    Y   N

11. I feel that the "culture" of my organization is just not me.
    Y   N

12. I feel overworked and underpaid.
    Y   N

13. I don't think I would enjoy doing the job my boss does.
    Y   N

14. I feel quite different from most people in my career field.
    Y   N

15. The career field I am in does not fit my interests.
    Y   N

16. I sometimes wonder if I will ever be a success in this career field.
    Y   N

17. I don't think I will ever earn the money I'd like to make in this career field.
    Y   N

18. I often daydream about trying out a new career field.
    Y   N

19. I never really put much thought into choosing this career in the first place.
    Y   N

20. I have a dissatisfaction with my career that I can't easily pinpoint.
    Y   N

Scoring:

First, count the number of times you responded Y. If you said Y to 15 or more of the statements, that may mean that both your current job and your overall career field are bugging you.

Next, look at where your Y responses are. If most of your Y responses were to statements 1 through 12, then you may need to think about changing employers, transferring to a different job with your current employer, or getting the same kind of job in a different industry or sector. (The main sectors of the work world are private/corporate, nonprofit, and government.) If you answered Y to most of statements 13 through 20, then a full career change may be in order for you.

Smart Move #214: Diagnose Your Career Crisis

If the results of the What's Bugging You Quiz indicate that the problem lies with anything other than your career field, then a full career change is probably not for you. In that case, you should go back to earlier chapters of this book to see what more you could be doing to improve your current situation. Sometimes, career dissatisfaction just lies with the job itself—your tasks, responsibilities, skills being used, or work schedule. It may relate to the people you work with or to the work environment—the physical space, rules, atmosphere, or dress code. The problem could also be with your employer's ethics, organizational culture, or management style. In that case, you don't necessarily need a whole new career—just a new job with a different company. The problem can also be situational due to organizational change, projects you have to work on temporarily, or working in an understaffed office or department. In those cases as well, you should not leave your job or career field until you've done everything you can to deal with the problem or ride out the change. (See chapter 5 for tips on dealing with organizational change.)

If, however, you found that the roots of your dissatisfaction are much deeper than something like a problem boss, annoying co-workers, disruptive organizational change, or any other fixable problem, then you may be looking at a career change as the answer to your dilemma. This diagnosis is an important step in laying the foundation for a career transition. Getting to the root of the problem helps you determine if a change is justified *and* helps you begin to define what you would want in your next career. Career dissatisfaction is a curable disease!

If you think that a career change is really what you need, think about whether you need:

(1) **A full career change** from one occupation, profession, or career field to another (e.g., going from being a paralegal to being a physical therapist, or going from being a teacher to being a banker).

(2) **A career shift** meaning a change of specialization within an occupation, profession, or career field (e.g., Veronica moving from a public relations agency to the public relations department of a corporation, or Jamie moving to marketing from direct sales).

(3) **An industry or sector change** in which your job title or area of specialization stays the same, but you move to a different sector of the labor market (e.g., Jamie staying within his functional area of sales but moving to a non-computer-related company, or Veronica moving from corporate public relations to a public relations position with a nonprofit organization).

Most of the smart moves in this chapter, as well as in chapters 7 and 8, address a full career change, but they can also apply to a career shift and an industry or sector change.

Smart Move #215: Begin a Career Change Journal

If you've never been the type to keep a daily diary or to record your every thought and move in a journal, don't worry. A career change journal is simply a record book where you make note of all the discoveries, thoughts, and plans for your career transition. It can be a spiral notebook, pad of paper, or file in your computer. The format is not so important as what goes into it. At this point, what you can put in it is your *career crisis diagnosis*. Simply record your thoughts on why you are dissatisfied with your current career and why a career change is justified. Then, using the three types of career changes defined in Smart Move #214 (full career change, career shift, or industry or sector change), write down in your journal exactly which type of career change you are seeking. These entries are an important step in that they not only keep your thoughts organized, but also provide a handy reference for later in the transition process. When you get deep into a career change, you are likely to have some second thoughts about whether you really want to go through with the transition (just about everyone does have at least *some* doubts). When that happens, you can look back at these early journal entries and remind yourself of what precipitated the change process.

AVOIDING THE COP-OUT

CHALLENGE: MAKING SURE YOU'RE NOT JUST TAKING THE EASY WAY OUT

When Veronica first mentioned to her parents and other family members and friends that she was thinking of getting out of public relations and into a whole new career field, some of them encouraged her to do so. But most felt that she shouldn't give up so quickly. Her parents, in particular, felt that she was just taking the easy way out. After hearing her talk for years about how she wanted to be a top executive with a prestigious public relations firm, they were taken aback by her sudden disinterest in her chosen career field. Veronica's parents thought she just needed more time to adjust to the politics of her large firm and that it would be a shame to fall off the fast-track toward that top job she had dreamed of. Some of her friends, too, couldn't understand why Veronica would want to leave a career that they saw as glamorous. Veronica knew deep down that a change was what she wanted and that the problem wasn't just with her specific job or employer. She had changed as a person since she was the twenty-one year old intern who was so enamored by public relations. She no longer felt that the career field fit with who she was. Veronica was convinced that a full career change was the right thing to do, but she didn't know how to convince her family and friends of that.

TAKING A LONG, HARD LOOK AT THE RATIONALE FOR YOUR CAREER CHANGE

When you're not happy, not doing well on your job, or don't seem to be getting anywhere in your career in general, it can be tempting to see a career change as a welcome panacea. Some people change careers simply because they see change as the easy way out. Changing career fields can be a way to avoid dealing with a difficult situation. Rather than confronting a problem boss or coworkers, changing your own behavior, negotiating for a new work schedule, looking for a new job, or transitioning to a new industry or sector, it can actually seem easier just to start over in a whole new career. Lots of people go back to school or take other fairly drastic steps to retrain or reposition themselves for a whole new occupation just to avoid dealing with a problem that *seems* overwhelming, but is really quite fixable. This faulty logic leads many people to bail out of careers that could have been rewarding and satisfying—if only they had been willing to ride out the rough spots.

A career change is not an easy process. It invariably takes time, effort, and even money (if retraining or further education is required). So, a career change is really not the easy way out. Like any kind of transition in life, a career change is a lot of work. If you decided in the last section of this chapter that a career change *is* the answer to your dilemma, then the smart moves that follow will serve as a sort of self-check mechanism. They'll help you make sure that you're being honest with yourself when you say that you need to change careers and will help you see if the effort that would have to go into a career transition is worth it to you.

Smart Move #216: Don't Assume Life is Better on the Other Side

If you're thinking of defecting to a whole other career world, ask yourself a tough question first: Am I assuming that life would be so much better in another career field, even though I don't have adequate data on which to base that assumption? When you hear about friends in other career fields or read about other professions, it's easy to succumb to the grass-is-greener syndrome. If you're unhappy in your present situation, then anything new and different can sound appealing. Be aware, though, that a career that's right for someone else may not be right for you. So, if you're tempted to change careers because some other career option seems more appealing, think twice. Don't make that assumption until you've investigated that option enough to know that it really is right for you. (Chapter 7 will show you ways to investigate your options and choose the right career.)

Smart Move #217: Distinguish Personal Problems from Professional Problems

When people are unhappy in their jobs or their career fields in general, that dissatisfaction can carry over into their life outside of work. If that's the case with you, then it may be necessary to change your career field before your dissatisfaction at work starts to have serious consequences. We have seen clients with physical and psychological difficulties, strained relationships, and other not-so-pleasant outcomes as a result of being in the wrong career or job.

Sometimes, though, just the opposite is happening, and that's what this smart move is all about: Problems in your personal life can seep into your professional life. This can lead to a desire for a career change that is actually masking a need for a change in your personal life. So, before assuming that the problem lies with your work, take a careful look at your life in general. Are there things you could be doing outside of work to make you feel more fulfilled and successful? Perhaps there are interests not being satisfied in your career that you could explore through classes, community service, or other activities. Are you bored with your social life or having difficulty in a relationship? Maybe you need to make some changes in those areas and keep your career as it is. Whatever your situation, take a candid look at your life as a whole before you assume that all your problems lie with your chosen career field.

Smart Move #218: Try to Make the Status Quo Work

Before deciding to take any drastic—or even not so drastic—action with your career, make sure that your current dissatisfaction is not temporary. You might be reacting, for example, to a disruptive work environment because of organizational restructuring or staff turnover. You might be experiencing burnout because you've been doing the same thing over and over ad nauseum. Or, you may be less than enthralled with some new responsibilities you've been given or with your coworkers. These are often fixable problems that do not require you to jump off your career track. So, before making a career change, see if there are things you could do to make your current situation better. Go back to the sources of dissatisfaction that you identified earlier in this chapter and consider ways to deal with those issues. (You may also benefit from revisiting parts one and two of this book to learn ways to make the status quo work.)

Smart Move #219: Get Input from Others

No major decision in life should be made alone. Even if you've always been able to trust your instincts and do the right thing, a career change is no time to test your self-sufficiency. Get input from trusted family and friends on whether a change makes sense for you. If any of them vetoes the idea, remember that they may not know you as well as you know yourself and may have out-dated or inaccurate knowledge about the world of work. If that's the case, then you don't necessarily have to follow their advice and give up on the idea of a career change. By the same token, don't just discount others' concerns without looking for some truth in what they're saying. They might point out an important issue in the decision that you had overlooked. In addition to family and friends, turn to people who may be in a better position to understand your career situation. Ask for input from professional colleagues whenever possible. (However, this may not be possible to do if you have to keep your interest in a possible career or job change confidential.) You might also want to think about turning to career development experts like career counselors or consultants who can help you evaluate the suitability of a career change in a careful manner.

CHANGE AS A NORM

Challenge: Seeing that it's okay to make a change

Veronica went through all the right initial steps in contemplating a career change. She identified the source of her dissatisfaction and found that it really was with the field of public relations in general. She also made sure she wasn't just taking the easy way out. As a result, she decided that a full career change was what she needed. There was a problem, though. No sooner had she come to that realization, when she started to get cold feet. Leaving her job and switching to a new career field seemed to go against everything she had ever been taught. Her parents had always pushed her to strive for a stable, secure career—something she could be happy and successful in for the rest of her life. They had never understood why she had already held jobs with three different firms in her short career. (She had tried to make them understand that changing jobs frequently is very common in a field like public relations, but they always responded with a lecture on the evils of "job-hopping.") Veronica knew in her gut that a career transition made sense for her, but the values her parents had tried to instill in her were holding her back—even though she knew those values were misguided in today's work climate.

Jamie also started to chicken-out when it became clear to him that a total career change was what he really wanted and needed. His hesitation grew primarily out of practical and logistical concerns. He had started to see that maybe he belonged on the technical side of the computer industry rather than in sales. The thought of being a programmer or software developer was exciting and intriguing, but it also had its downside. Qualifying for those areas would mean going back to school for the necessary training and would also mean that the road to high earnings would be much longer than if he stayed in sales. Like Veronica, Jamie knew deep down that a career change did make sense for him. He realized that all the money in the world wouldn't be enough if he hated going to a sales job everyday. And, even if he could stomach sales, there was no guarantee that he'd be making the big bucks. As a career counselor had pointed out to him, Jamie's chances for success in sales were not too high if the career wasn't right for him in the first place. So, all signs pointed toward getting out of sales and into something that he was already gravitating toward naturally, based on his true interests and innate talents. Despite these clear signs, though, Jamie wondered if he was crazy to be abandoning a potentially lucrative, high-powered career track.

RETHINKING THE WAY YOU VIEW CAREERS

Just about everyone who considers making a career transition at some point faces the same concerns and fears as Jamie and Veronica faced. It's perfectly normal to hesitate before you make a big move. The hesitation probably comes from some primordial self-preservation mechanism that keeps us from doing really stupid things with our lives. So, if you're wondering whether it's okay to make a change, be glad you are wondering. If you weren't, then you'd probably be going into this transition with blinders on. The following three smart moves will help you see career change as a norm—not as an anomaly. You'll see that, if handled carefully, a career change will not do any harm to your professional reputation or chances for success. It really is okay to change careers!

Smart Move #220: Consider How the World of Work Has Changed

If you've read a single magazine or newspaper, watched television, or listened to the radio in the past few years, it probably comes as no surprise for you to hear that the work world has changed exponentially in the 1990's. In fact, it's become almost a cliché to talk about "the dramatic changes in the labor market" or "the restructuring of the workplace." You may have seen your parents laid off from what they thought were stable jobs. You may have watched older siblings or friends struggle to land jobs in a tight market. Or, you might have experienced these problems yourself. The shrinking of opportunities in the corporate world, the reorganization in other sectors, and the fluctuating economy have all been wake-up calls for people trying to manage their careers successfully since the early 1990s.

Things are looking up, however, as we round out the decade. Jobs are somewhat more plentiful, downsizing in big corporations has become less common, and the economy seems to be stronger. Despite these improvements, though, one remnant of the tumultuous work world described above does remain. That remnant is a new attitude about careers.

Because people from all walks of life and all levels of their careers were forced to make changes during the recent tumultuous period, a new set of norms for career development was established. In an era of organizational downsizing and economic recession, enormous numbers of people saw their carefully planned careers go haywire. Many found that they had to change career fields because they just couldn't find jobs in the field they had been in. As a result, new norms were established. It became commonplace to make career transitions, whether just from one employer to another, or from one whole occupation to another. What this means is that it really is okay for you to consider changing careers. Doing so is not looked upon as the flaky, unprofessional, or irresponsible move that it would have been considered when your parents, grandparents, or even older siblings were in their twenties and thirties.

Career Change As a Norm

Whether you're reading official statistics from the U.S. Department of Labor, talking to experienced career counselors or outplacement consultants, or just listening to the guy down the hall from you spout opinions, just about everyone agrees that the average person these days changes careers at least three to five times in a lifetime. Some of those are just career shifts or changes of specialization—not full career field changes. Either way, career changes have become the norm rather than the exception in most people's career development.

Smart Move #221: Learn the New Definition of Career Satisfaction

Another result of the changes in the work world over the past several years is that many people have redefined what career satisfaction means to them. A satisfying career used to be one which offered some sense of job security, a steady paycheck, and an employer that would look out for you. The new attitude is something like,

> *"If my employer can't guarantee me job security, and if I'm likely to be overworked and underpaid, then I may as well at least enjoy the actual work I'm doing."*

Most people these days really want to like their jobs and their careers. That may sound painfully obvious, but it wasn't always the case. If you're in your twenties or thirties, you may have seen your parents (or grandparents, or other relatives) spend years toiling away in a career they didn't particularly enjoy. They may have done so out of a sense of duty or a need to earn a certain amount of money or to appear respectable and diligent to the rest of society. The generation making their way in the work world today has a different set of expectations. Chances are, you want more out of your career. You want to enjoy, and feel good about, what you're doing. There's nothing wrong with that! If you have to change career fields to find that satisfaction, then by all means, do so.

The Class of 2000 Looks for Satisfaction Outside of the Corporate World

The Annual Freshman Survey conducted by UCLA's Higher Education Research Institute (a survey of a whopping 250,000 college freshmen nationwide) found striking differences in the career orientation of the Class of 2000 as compared to previous freshmen in the study's thirty-one year history. In the fall of 1996, freshmen entering college expressed more interest in teaching careers than any entering class had in the past twenty-three years. This group also expressed a record low interest in careers in law and the lowest interest in business careers in twenty years. These freshmen were also the most community service-minded group in the survey's history.

Smart Move #222: Remove the Term *Job-Hopping* from Your Vocabulary

Job-hopping has traditionally meant going from job to job without staying in any one place long enough to get the seat warm. Some people consider staying at a job less than a year to be job-hopping, while others are a little more lenient and only call you a job-hopper if you leave after six months or less. While it never hurts to stick it out for a nice even year, there are plenty of times when leaving before a year is up is warranted. One of those times is when you're changing career fields.

Say you're in marketing and decide you want to become a veterinarian. That's a pretty major career change that's going to involve years of graduate school and internships before you can get your first job as a vet. So when you do apply for a job as a vet, no one is going to care that you left your last job in marketing after only a few months. Your pregrad school resume will hardly even be looked at. What will be of more interest to prospective employers is what you've done in terms of work experience and school since you made the decision to become a vet.

But, what if your career transition is less dramatic and time-consuming than going from something like marketing to veterinary work? Well, even then, the same rationale applies. Say you're still staying in the corporate world but just moving from marketing to sales, and you leave your marketing job after a few months. All you have to say to justify the move is that, after careful consideration, you realized you wanted to be in sales and that you needed to leave your job to devote all your time and attention to making the transition. (You may have needed time to take a class in sales techniques, network with people in sales, do research, and look for a sales job.) You can also point out that it was the considerate way to treat your employer. No one wants to work with someone who has one foot out the door. So, whatever your specific situation, job-hopping is not likely to apply to you. When you make a career change, you start with something of a clean slate. While your employment history *is* relevant, it's not the most critical factor in a career change.

CHAPTER 7

Finding the Best New Career for You

WORK SMART IQ QUIZ #7

Review each item below and decide if it's a work smart myth or a work smart reality. In the space before each statement, put an M if you think it's a myth and an R if you think it's a reality. Then check your responses with the correct answers at the end of the quiz.

_____ **1.** To be happy, you don't necessarily have to incorporate all—or even any—of your interests into your career choice.

_____ **2.** Identifying your skills isn't that important because they mainly reflect your abilities in your old career, not your new one.

_____ **3.** Altruism, creativity, status, and personal interaction are examples of values that may be important to someone in a career choice.

_____ **4.** Sometimes you must make hard choices among your top interests, skills, and values when making a career decision.

_____ 5. Thinking about what you *don't* want in a career is a waste of time. You really just need to focus on what you do want.

_____ 6. Reading and talking to people are two key ways to research career possibilities.

_____ 7. You should find out what the hot careers are for the next decade and make a career choice based on them, even if they don't quite match your top interests, skills, and values.

_____ 8. Your options are limited if you don't want to pursue the traditional professions, (law, medicine, and business).

_____ 9. Sometimes you need to bridge a gap in skills, experience, or educational training before you can make a transition into your new career field.

_____ 10. When you're narrowing down your career choice options, follow your instincts and also use a systematic decision-making approach.

Answers: (1)-R, (2)-M, (3)-R, (4)-R, (5)-M, (6)-R, (7)-M, (8)-M, (9)-R, (10)-R

CHANGE CRITERIA

CHALLENGE: DECIDING WHAT YOU REALLY WANT OUT OF THIS CAREER MOVE

Courtney had worked in a bank for a few years since college. She was in a customer service role, helping the bank's existing clients and also establishing new accounts. Although Courtney was up for a promotion to assistant manager, and the talk around the office was that she would definitely get the position, she had decided to leave banking. Courtney had always had a creative streak and longed for a career that would make use of her artistic abilities. She was concerned, however, that some of the careers that interested her, like interior design and freelance illustrating, might not be lucrative or stable enough. Courtney knew she would be good at them, though, and that they would also offer her some autonomy— something she thought might be a priority for her. Courtney realized that there were also some other areas of commercial arts she could go into which might be more lucrative and offer more traditional full-time employment opportunities, (e.g., graphic design in an advertising agency, or package design for a manufacturing firm). But Courtney worried that those careers might not be as interesting to her or offer the autonomy and flexibility she wanted. She knew that, in order to decide among all the creative career options, she would need to establish some priorities for her career change. Courtney just wasn't sure how to do so.

DEFINING THE FACTORS TO BASE YOUR CAREER CHOICE ON

A career change is a big step—one that often involves considerable time, effort, and maybe even money to implement. It is therefore critical to choose the right field. You want to make sure that your effort is worthwhile, and that your new career comes much closer to offering the satisfaction and success you were lacking before. The best way to make a careful career decision is to first define what you need in your next career, then to generate specific career options through research and networking, and finally, to use decision-making techniques to choose among those options. Those last two steps are discussed later in this chapter. For now, we'll look at smart moves that help you define what you want out of your next career.

Smart Move #223: Identify Your Interests

Your interests are the things you enjoy doing, thinking about, talking about, or reading about. They might be all out passions (interests that are an integral part of your identity) or might just be casual interests you pursue occasionally. They may be long-standing interests you've had for years or just passing fancies—nothing to base a career choice on.

While it's great to go into a career field that actually interests you, you don't necessarily have to incorporate all, or even any, of your interests into your career choice. Some people have jobs that don't reflect their true passions but that offer something else, like a high salary, or a convenient location or schedule. If you do end up choosing a career field that doesn't involve your top interests, remember that there are lots of other ways to satisfy your interests. The goal is to figure out which interests are strong enough to make a career out of, and are feasible enough to incorporate into your career. When you've thought about what some of your interests are, make note of them in your career change journal.

Creative Ways to Clue into Your Real Interests

- *Imagine that you won the lottery but decided to continue working. What kind of work would you do?*
- *What are your favorite things to read? Is there a pattern to the type of things you read?*
- *What topics interest you enough to stay up half the night discussing them with friends?*
- *If you had lots of money to contribute to charities or other causes, to whom would you give your money?*
- *During which kinds of activities or projects do you get so engrossed that you lose track of time?*
- *Which jobs or internships in your work history were most interesting to you?*
- *What are your favorite ways to spend your free time?*

Smart Move #224: Identify the Skills You Want to Use

When making a career choice, it's best to think of skills in a fairly broad way. The category of skills can include a number of factors, including actual tangible skills you've acquired as well as more innate talents, aptitudes, strengths, and capabilities. You can think of your skills as being those things that come easily for you or that you know you could master and do effectively. Skills are especially important when changing careers because these are the selling points you bring with you—the transferable skills that show employers in your new field that your abilities aren't limited to what you did in your old career.

To determine which skills should be a factor in the career choice you're trying to make, refer to the lists in the Hot Competencies and Special Skills Exercises in chapter 4. Then, take out your career change journal and make note of at least five competencies or skills you possess now that you would like to use in your new career. Be sure you're listing ones *that you would like to use*, not just any old skills or competencies that you possess. You might be good at something that you don't particularly enjoy doing. Also make a list of the skills or competencies that you'd like to develop in your new career. (List as many as you'd like.)

Smart Move #225: Identify Your Work-Related Values

Your work-related values are the things that are important to you. You can think of them as needs. They're the qualities that a career field needs to have in order for you to feel satisfied in it. Values can be intrinsic needs, like having the opportunity for creative expression, intellectual stimulation, or altruism in your work. Or, values can be extrinsic factors, like the type of work environment you want, the income level you need, or a particular work schedule.

If you do work that does not satisfy your values, then you're likely to be unhappy. It's important, therefore, to clarify your values as best you can before choosing a career. The Values Checklist that follows shows many typical values that people often need in their work. This exercise will force you to clarify what is really important to you.

VALUES CHECKLIST

Read through the following list of work-related values and rate how important each is to you in your work life (not in your personal life). Use a scale from 1 to 4, with 1 being extremely important and 4 being not at all important. Write your rating for each value in the check-box provided next to it.

☐ ALTRUISM (broad)—Do work that contributes to helping society.

☐ ALTRUISM (specific)—Do work that helps others directly, in groups or one-on-one.

☐ DECISION-MAKING—Have the power and responsibility for making decisions on the job.

☐ POWER AND AUTHORITY—Have control over other people or projects.

☐ INTELLECTUAL STIMULATION—Deal with intellectually challenging tasks on the job.

☐ STATUS (intellectual)—Be seen as someone who is especially knowledgeable and has a high level of expertise in a particular field.

☐ STATUS (general)—Be regarded as someone who holds a prestigious position.

☐ ARTISTIC EXPRESSION—Have the opportunity to produce, or be involved in the production of, artistic works on the job.

☐ CREATIVITY—Create new ideas, programs, designs, or systems on the job.

☐ AESTHETICS —Have the opportunity to be surrounded by, study, or appreciate things of beauty on the job.

☐ MANAGEMENT—Be responsible for supervising or overseeing people or projects.

☐ VISIBILITY—Be widely recognized for the quality or nature of my work or simply be a visible person in my field.

☐ EXCITEMENT—Experience excitement, unpredictability, or adventure in my work.

☐ PHYSICAL ACTIVITY—Work that lets me be challenged physically (or at least move around a lot).

☐ PEOPLE INTERACTION—Have the opportunity to interact extensively with people as a routine part of my work.

☐ COMPETITIVE ENVIRONMENT—Work in a competitive office, organization, or career field.

☐ CASUAL ENVIRONMENT—Work in an office, organization, or career field that is informal and low-key.

☐ ADVANCEMENT—Have ample opportunity to be promoted or to take on increasing responsibility.

☐ VARIETY—Have a job where the content or setting of my work changes frequently.

☐ STABILITY—Have a work routine or schedule that is fairly predictable.

- [ ] JOB SECURITY—Know that my employment is as secure as possible and that my overall career field offers plenty of job opportunities.

- [ ] AUTONOMY—Be able to determine the nature of my work and my work routine.

- [ ] INDEPENDENCE—Work primarily on my own rather than in groups.

- [ ] TIME FLEXIBIITY—Be able to schedule my work according to my own preferences rather than having rigidly set hours.

Now, look back over the values you rated with 1s or 2s and circle the values that are of utmost importance to you. (Try to circle no more than five.)

Ways to Assess Your Interests, Skills, and Values

- *Take vocational tests administered by a qualified career counselor.*
- *Complete self-assessment exercises provided in many popular career guidebooks like the ones listed in the Choosing Careers section of this book's bibliography.*
- *Ask people who know you well what they think your interests, strengths, and values are.*
- *Think about what made you happy and what you did particularly well in past jobs, internships, volunteer experiences, or class projects.*
- *To assess skills, try to remember (or look back through past performance reviews) to see what your past or current supervisors and peers have commended you for.*
- *Simply make a list of the top ten things you like, do well, and consider to be important.*

Smart Move #226: Define Your Priorities

This Smart Move is the positive spin on the earlier smart moves that involved identifying what you don't like about your current job or career field. Now, instead of looking at what's wrong, you're looking for what could be right.

Think about your interests, skills, and values and make a list in your career change journal of the top five to seven in each category. Then look at your lists and find the top three to five factors from across all three lists. These are your priorities. Write them in your career change journal.

Smart Move #227: Know What You Want to Avoid

This is the opposite of your priorities. What do you absolutely not want in your next career? The things you want to avoid might be based on what you've hated about your current or past career fields or specific jobs. You can also get ideas of what to avoid by looking at what you want and thinking of what the opposite of that would be. For values, you can look back at the Values Checklist in Smart Move #225 and find the values that you rated as 4s. If you feel strongly about these, they might go onto the list of things that you want to avoid. Also, look back at the skills lists to find the skills you have or could develop but don't want to use. To find what you want to avoid in the interests category, think of the things you have absolutely no interest in. These might go on your avoidance list. When you've come up with several things that you want to avoid, write them in your career change journal.

Smart Move #228: Paint a Picture of Your Ideal Career

Now that you've identified your priorities and thought about what you want to avoid, you should be starting to get a picture of your ideal career. To get this rough image down on paper, the Career Change Criteria Worksheet is provided. It will help you pull all your self-assessment data together to form one brief profile of what your next career should look like. You won't necessarily be able to identify any suitable occupational titles or job titles for yourself yet. At this point you have just a rough sketch of the occupation, i.e., career field, or job that you should go into. You'll be able to fill in the details of that rough sketch after you take the smart moves in the Generating Options section that follows.

For now you just need to get these criteria down so that you can start to brainstorm careers that match your criteria. Writing down the criteria in one brief profile also gives you something to refer to when you research career options (as described in the next section). You will use the career change criteria to evaluate whether various career options fit with what you're looking for, or should be avoided.

Career Change Criteria Worksheet

The most important things I want in my next career are:

_____	_____
_____	_____
_____	_____

The skills and competencies I most want to use or develop in my next career are:

_____	_____
_____	_____
_____	_____
_____	_____
_____	_____

The interests I would like to incorporate in my next career are:

_____	_____
_____	_____

The values I need satisfied in my next career are:

_____	_____
_____	_____
_____	_____

What I absolutely want to avoid in my next career is:

_____	_____
_____	_____
_____	_____

GENERATING OPTIONS

CHALLENGE: FINDING OUT WHAT'S OUT THERE

Courtney had some idea of the creative or artistic careers that she could choose from if she wanted to leave banking, but she knew there must be others out there that she wasn't aware of or was forgetting about. She worried that she was only thinking of the obvious options or the careers that she knew about because she had friends and family working in them. Courtney wished that there were an easy way to learn about every possible career option so that she could make a well-informed decision.

RESEARCHING THE WORK WORLD

There *is* a way to find out what's out there. It involves using print and on-line resources that are easy to get a hold of, as well as talking to people who can educate you about the work world in general or specific career fields within it. If you are thorough and methodical in your research, you will be able to come up with career options you didn't even know existed, as well as useful information on ones you were already aware of. The smart moves that follow will help you learn to survey the work world.

SMART MOVE #229: RESEARCHING YOUR WAY TO A NEW CAREER

A thorough process of career research can help you survey the work world and find the right career for you. This process can take you anywhere from two days to two years to complete, depending on how much time you want to put into it.

You can think of your research as involving two steps. The first is reading. There are many guidebooks, found in the career section of bookstores and in public or school libraries, that give you an overview of various career fields. Some of these are listed in the Researching Careers section of the bibliography in the appendix.

You can also read about careers in sources that aren't intended as career guides, but end up serving that purpose. Reading business magazines, for example, informs you about different careers in the business world. Reading a daily newspaper that has sections on science news, the arts, politics, and other topics can educate you about careers in those areas. Even if an article is not written with a focus on careers, you can often infer career information from it. The help-wanted ads in newspapers are also good ways to explore what's out there, long before you're ready to use those ads for actual job search purposes. Many career-related Web sites can also educate you about what careers are out there and what they entail. We've listed many of these in the Recommended Web Sites section of the Appendix.

In addition to reading about careers, you need to talk to people as well. Use some of the networking techniques suggested in chapters 3 and 5 to make contact with people who could help you learn about your options. Talking to people who know about many different career fields, or who have in-depth knowledge of one specific field is a great way to get a reality-based picture of your career choices. Just be sure that you balance the talking to people with some basic, objective information from reading as well.

Smart Move #230: Zero In On the Growth Careers

As you read or talk to people about the work world, you will undoubtedly come across the terms *growth careers* or *hot careers*. The U.S. Department of Labor and other entities make annual and quarterly projections about which fields will have the most jobs opening up in the coming years. This can be valuable data to have if you are particularly concerned about job security. It can also be handy to know about if you listed excitement or variety as one of your top values in Smart Move #225. Many of the growth careers offer plenty in the way of adventure since that's where innovation and change is likely to be taking place.

Be aware, though, that just because a career field is hot doesn't mean you should necessarily go into it. It still has to be right for you overall. If you choose a career just because some statistical report says that it is a growth field, you might end up making a mistake. You need to make sure that the career fits with the career change criteria you listed on your worksheet in Smart Move #228. If it also happens to be a growing area, then that's just icing on the cake.

Most projections on career growth come out of the Department of Labor or Bureau of Labor Statistics. Libraries typically keep their quarterly and annual reports on file. Also, many guidebooks like those listed in the Researching Careers section of the bibliography discuss the outlook for various fields.

Hot Careers for the Future

According to Martin Yate, career development expert and author of Career Smarts: Jobs with a Future (Ballantine Books/Random House, 1997), the two fastest growing industries—and specific areas within those industries—are:

Health Care
- *Health Administration*
- *Nursing*
- *Physical Health*
- *Dentistry*
- *Mental Health*

The Technologies
- *Biotechnology*
- *Environmental Technology*
- *Engineering*
- *Information Technology*

Smart Move #231: Consider an Offbeat Option

As you do your career research, you're most likely to read and hear about the more traditional career fields. You can easily find out everything you ever wanted to know about careers in business, law, and medicine. But what if you're not interested in those things? If you think that you want something a little different, don't despair. There are plenty of interesting opportunities available to you. You have more choices than you might realize: For example, you can build houses in Central America, teach English in Japan, or learn stained-glass-making in Italy. There are established programs like the Peace Corps and Americorps available to you, or you can get creative and craft something of your own design. College or university career centers and public libraries are the best sources of information on the not-so-mainstream options.

With a few exceptions, these options are not just limited to recent college grads. Even if you've been working full time for a while, you do have the option to take time out from the traditional professional track. Doing so is especially helpful if you are feeling burned out and don't think you're in the right state of mind to make a good, long-term career choice. *Voluntary downshifting* is the term that's been coined by demographers for the 1990s trend of getting off the fast track to do something you'll find fulfilling and rejuvenating.

Smart Move #232: Consider an Interim Option

When making a career change, there are times when you need to take an interim job before you can move fully into the new field you've chosen. You might not have the skills or experience you need or may need to go back to school for further educational credentials. In those cases, it can take some time (anywhere from a couple of months to a matter of years) to bridge the gap between your old field and the new one. Sometimes you can engage in those gap-bridging activities part time while still working in your current job, but you may need to leave your job to devote more time and energy to moving into your new career. In that case, an interim option may be the answer. Depending on what is feasible for you financially (and psychologically), and what your skills are, interim jobs might be working in a restaurant, working as a sales clerk in a retail store, being an intern in your new target career area, or doing temporary work. If you want an interim job of a higher caliber, you might look at ways that you could work as a consultant or freelancer in your current field.

Smart Move #233: Consider the Solo Route

Small business is one of the fastest-growing sectors of our economy. Businesses that employ less than about fifty people, experts offering their services as consultants or freelancers, and professionals going into private practice, are all becoming increasingly common.

Encouraging Facts about Small Business

- There are over 22 million small businesses in the U.S.
- In recent years, small businesses have accounted for about 75% of all new jobs created in the U.S.
- Small businesses employ 53% of the private work force.
- Small businesses produce 55% of all product innovations and produce twice as many product innovations per employee as large firms.

Source: The Facts About Small Business, 1996, Office of Advocacy, U.S. Small Business Administration

---

So, in surveying your options for a career change, you might want to consider taking the solo route—being your own boss. If you listed autonomy or independence and time freedom or flexibility among your career change criteria, then the entrepreneurial route may be for you. If you start your own business or become a consultant or freelancer, you're likely to work harder than you ever did when employed by someone else, but at least you know the effort is

all for your own venture. Being self-employed can be highly rewarding, but it is also risky and incredibly hard work. So, don't go
jumping into self-employment just because it's a growing area.
Give it some careful thought first. (Many of the books listed in the
Self-Employment section of the Appendix can help you decide if the
entrepreneurial track is right for you, and if so, how to go about
getting there.)

**Great Web Sites for Info on Small and Home-
Based Businesses**

The American Home Business Association
www.homebusiness.com

American Individual Magazine
http://aimc.com

Gil Gordon Associates
http://www.gilgordon.com

Business at Home
www.gohome.com

Home Business Journal
www.homebizjour.com

Small & Home-Based Business Links
www.ro.com/small_business/homebased.html

The U.S. Small Business Administration
www.sbaonline.sba.gov

About Work
www.aboutwork.com

CHOOSING

CHALLENGE: CHOOSING THE BEST CAREER OUT OF ALL THE POSSIBLE OPTIONS

Courtney was diligent in researching career options in creative
fields. She read a great deal, talked to many people, sat in on
Internet newsgroup chats about different careers, and collected information from professional associations and art schools. Courtney
was able to rule out some career choices because they didn't fit
enough of her criteria, but she was still left with a long list of
options. Some days she looked at her list and thought everything
sounded great, while other days she found so many things wrong
with each option that she wondered if she'd ever find the right
career. How would she ever decide?

Finding a Match Between What You Want and What's Out There

When it comes time to make an actual career choice, the way to approach it is to maintain the deliberate, methodical methods you used to identify your change criteria and research your options. Now is not the time to panic, feeling that the answer should be coming to you in a vision. You still have some work to do before you make your choice. That work involves weighing the results of your research with what you know are your career change criteria. It is a systematic process of evaluating your various career options until you zero in on the one that best matches your criteria. And, of course, what your gut instincts tell you is the right career has a role here too.

Smart Move #234: Don't Just Follow the Flock

The most important first step in making a good career choice is to adopt an independent frame of mind. You'll want to make sure that the direction you decide to head in is what you really want to be doing. Too many people make career choices based on what they think others expect of them or on what seems to be the thing to do these days. (For example, just because we mentioned in a previous smart move that the solo route is an increasingly popular career choice doesn't mean you ought to rush out and start your own business.) You shouldn't necessarily head for a particular career just because your research revealed that it's rated as one of the top growth fields for the twenty-first century either. If options aren't right for you, then you shouldn't go for them—no matter how trendy they are. You also shouldn't let other people's opinions sway you too much. Even though it's important to get others' input on what might be a good career choice for you, no one but yourself can tell you what you really want to do.

Smart Move #235: Revisit Your Change Criteria

Before you start to evaluate each of your career options, it's helpful to look back over your Career Change Criteria Worksheet in Smart Move #228 to see if that profile of the ideal career still makes sense to you. You might want to adjust some of the career change criteria that you listed there. Sometimes when you research the world of work, you end up rethinking your priorities. If you found, for example, that it seems there's no career that will let you avoid what you thought you were determined to avoid, then you may need to lower your expectations just a bit. Or, if you found that it's just about impossible for all of your priorities to be met in any one career, then you may need to think about which priorities are most important.

Smart Move #236: Systematically Evaluate Your Options

Here's where you actually get to the point of choosing the best career field for you. The way to do that is to see how each option you're considering meets the career change criteria you have identified. You will need to rely on what you've learned in your research phase in order to determine how each career measures up. The chart below is one way to ensure that you are systematic and objective in your evaluation of each option.

My Best Career Option Chart

List all of the career options that you're deciding among in the column down the left side of the page under the heading "Career Options." (You should have narrowed down your options to no more than five careers at this point.) Then, consider how each of those options matches your overall priorities, the skills you want to use, your interests, values, and the things you want to avoid. Place a plus (+) or a minus (-) in each column to reflect how each career option stacks up in each category. Then look at which career comes closest to matching all of your career change criteria.

Career Options	Priorities	Skills	Interests	Values	Avoidance Factors
1.					
2.					
3.					
4.					
5.					

Smart Move #237: Take a Reality Check

Once you've narrowed your options to the one best career for you, make sure that the career really makes sense for you. When you've taken a systematic approach to making a career decision, you'll usually make a good one, but there is a potential downside to that careful approach. The downside is that you can make a choice that looks good on paper, but for some reason doesn't make sense in reality. You might, for example, have overlooked one big factor like the cost of training to get into that career or where you would have to live to get jobs in that field. Or, you might have taken all relevant factors into account, but you weren't realistic in considering how much of a barrier they might be. When you were at the research stage, for example, you might have said, "Graduate school looks expensive, but I'm sure I can figure out a way to pay for it if it's necessary for getting into this field." Or, "I see that this career requires people to be really outgoing and I'm more of an introvert, but I'm sure that I can change." Sure, there are lots of creative ways to pay for grad school, and introverts can push themselves to be a little more outgoing, but just be sure you aren't setting yourself up for disaster by making statements like these. The career decision-making process is not time to be living in a fantasy land.

Another case for rethinking your choice is that you might have taken all important factors into account and been realistic about them, but you just find that the whole doesn't really equal the sum of its parts. What that means is that, when analyzing a career option by picking it apart and evaluating its features against your change criteria (like you did in the My Best Career Option Chart), you might lose sight of the big picture. You might find that what makes sense on a checklist or chart doesn't make sense in reality. The career you end up choosing just might not sit right. Your gut or your heart may tell you it's simply not the right direction for you to head. Career choices, like any decision, should be based on a combination of objective and subjective decision-making tactics. In other words, how you feel about a career option is just as important as what you think about it.

Just be sure, though, that you don't go only with your feelings. You need to be cautious about listening to your feelings too much because they may be reflecting your concern about a career change in general, not just a specific career option. You might, for example, end up deciding on a particular career direction, then have serious doubts about whether or not it's right for you. Those doubts may have very little to do with that actual career choice but might instead be a reflection of fears you have about making a career change at all. Change of any sort can bring about feelings of anxiety in many people, so before you assume that your hesitation is related to your specific choice, think about the possibility that you might just be hesitant about making any choice. (Ways to deal with these fears are discussed in chapter 8.)

So, be sure that when you let feelings enter into a career decision, you are sure where those feelings are really coming from. Also make sure that you rely just as much on what your head tells you is right as what your heart or gut tells you. A career choice that's not based on some logical, systematic research and evaluation process is likely to be the wrong choice. So, start with the steps previously described in this chapter, then trust your instincts about what really feels right.

8

Making the Transition

WORK SMART IQ QUIZ #8

Review each item below and decide if it's a work smart myth or a work smart reality. In the space before each statement, put an M if you think it's a myth and an R if you think it's a reality. Then check your responses with the correct answers at the end of the quiz.

_____ 1. When you want to make a career change, you must quit your job and devote yourself full time to making the transition.

_____ 2. It's a good idea to make a career transition game plan that breaks the process into mini-transitions with specific goals and deadlines for each one.

_____ 3. Announce your intended career change to people in your work and personal lives only when it's necessary, finalized, and—if possible—underway.

_____ 4. Give your family and friends as little detail as possible about how and why you made your career change decision.

_____ 5. Talk about your change with your current employer and colleagues to gain their respect before you leave your current job.

_____ 6. Research the best ways to get ready for your transition (e.g., do a job search, revamp your resume, retool your image, apply to graduate school, or start a business) before you jump in.

_____ 7. Even if you graduated a while ago, your alma mater can be a useful resource for preparing to make a career change.

_____ 8. Accept that you may have to take a moderate pay cut or stay at your present salary to land your first job in a new field.

_____ 9. It's important to show your friends, family, and others that you're competent during a career transition by handling the practical and emotional challenges independently.

_____ 10. If you make a career change and hate it, get out right away and do something completely different so that you don't get depressed.

Answers: (1)-M, (2)-R, (3)-R, (4)-M, (5)-M, (6)-R, (7)-R, (8)-R, (9)-M, (10)-M

TIMING

CHALLENGE: KNOWING WHEN TO MAKE A MOVE

Madeleine, an accountant in her early thirties, was tired of working for other people, so she decided to start her own business . She had realized that the rapid growth in the entrepreneurial sector of the economy meant that more and more small businesses and independent consultants would be needing accounting services. So, she decided to start a business services company which would handle payroll administration, tax preparation, basic bookkeeping, and related accounting services. Madeleine would also serve as a consultant to entrepreneurs, showing them how to set up in-house systems for those functions, rather than having her company handle the procedures. Madeleine was excited about getting her business started but wasn't sure when she should do so. Some people said she should stay in her job with the accounting firm for a while and start her own company on the side slowly. Others said the only way to get it going was to take the plunge and go into full-time self-employment. Madeleine didn't know which timing made the most sense.

Craig also had questions about the timing of his career change—not because he was going into self-employment but because he was making a full career change and had a lot of options for how to go about it. Craig was an English teacher in his late twenties who had decided he wanted to become a documentary film maker. His transition would involve going to film school for an M.F.A. and also trying to get entry-level production assistant jobs for some hands-on experience. Unfortunately, he had made the decision about his career change in the summer when it was too late to apply for graduate programs that fall. He wasn't sure if he should go back to teaching in the fall and wait to apply for the following year's graduate school class, or if he should not return to teaching and try instead to get a job related to film, then apply to school for the following year.

PLANNING A TRANSITION STRATEGY

Craig and Madeleine faced the typical dilemma that most career changers encounter. In order to make the right decisions about quitting your job, going back to school, or starting a business, you need to devise a strategy that will work. The strategy should be based primarily on what you learned during the research phase of your career planning (as described in chapter 7), as well as on an understanding of the change process in general.

Smart Move #238: Understand Change as a Process

Patience is very important when it comes to making a career change. No matter how eager you are to get going with your new endeavor, you need to think twice before handing in your resignation, enrolling in school, or setting up shop in your own business. All transitions are made up of mini-transitions. So, instead of looking at your career change as one big event that you can mark on the calendar, break the change process down into steps.

At the same time, you should be realistic about what those steps should be. Many career changes require that you spend some time bridging the gap between what you've been doing and what you need to be doing. Whether you need to go to graduate school for several years or simply need to spend a couple of months networking with people in your new field in preparation for getting a job, it's important to allow time to do it. Career changes cannot, and should not, be rushed.

Smart Move #239: Evaluate Your Options

A next step in determining the timing of your move is to evaluate the viability and feasibility of your transition options. Those options usually include:

- Staying in your current job until you find a job in your new field.

- Staying in your current job while bridging the gap to qualify for your new field (e.g., taking classes part time, doing volunteer or project-based work, developing new skills, networking, etc.)

- Leaving your job so you can bridge the gap full time.

- Leaving your job so you can search for a new job full time.

- Leaving your job but working in an interim job (that may be unrelated to both your old and new career field) while pursuing gap-bridging activities part time.

Similar options would apply if your career change is to an entrepreneurial endeavor. You could start a new business on the side while staying in your current job or could get an interim full- or part-time job while starting the new business slowly on the side. You could remain in your current job and simply lay the foundation for your business—preparing a business plan, securing office space or setting up a home office, doing some initial marketing, etc. Then, when all the preliminary steps were in place, you could leave your job and go into business full time.

The options you choose for your transition timing will most likely be based on the nature and magnitude of the change you're making, your current and projected financial situation, and your attitude toward risk-taking. Be sure to take all of these factors into account as you evaluate your timing options.

Smart Move #240: Anticipate the Consequences of Your Move

Speaking of risk-taking, a second way to evaluate your options is to look at the possible negative consequences of each move you could make. When evaluating the timing options listed in Smart Move #239, think about bad things that could happen if you went with each option. Don't just think about the potentially disastrous consequences, either. Try to estimate the moderately negative or the minor damaging ones as well. To determine whether a consequence would be less than positive, take into account how it would affect you financially, personally, or professionally.

Smart Move #241: Establish a Transition Game Plan

To plot a course for your career change, it's important to put together a workable plan. One way to do this is to take out your career change journal and write down all the mini-steps involved in your career transition. (If you don't know what these steps are, then you probably don't know enough about the career field or business you're heading into. In that case, you need to go back to talking to people and doing research as was recommended in chapter 7.)

Next, think about how long each step will take (Be realistic!) or when a deadline would be for each step (as in deadlines for applying to school or training programs). Based on those calculations, assign blocks of time during which you'll take care of each step and mark those on a calendar or in your appointment book. The time periods you allot might be a day, several weeks, a few months, or even a year or more. The length depends on how much is involved in each mini-step.

ANNOUNCING

Challenge: Making Sure News of Your Career Change Is Well Received

Craig decided to take a fairly cautious route to his new career endeavors. He decided to go back to teaching for one more academic year and to enroll in continuing education classes in filmmaking to bolster his future application for graduate school.

He also arranged to volunteer his time on weekends, handling office work for a small production company. His timing would mean that he'd have a pretty heavy schedule for the coming year, but he knew it was the best way to proceed.

He was concerned, however, about when and how he should announce his planned career change to people—both colleagues in the education field and his personal network of friends and family. He was worried that his friends and family would try to talk him out of going into film. As for colleagues at his school, he suspected that he should keep his evening and weekend activities in film a secret so that their perception of him as a fully committed English teacher would not change. Craig worried, though, that some conflicts in his schedule would come up (e.g., needing to participate in after-school or weekend activities with teachers or students when he needed to be at film class or in his weekend job). In that case, it might be hard to keep his outside activities confidential.

TAKING SITUATIONAL AND PEOPLE FACTORS INTO ACCOUNT

One of the most difficult aspects of a career change is often the process of announcing the news of your impending change to other people, both in your personal and professional life. The smart moves that follow can make the announcement less of a nerve-racking and potentially damaging experience for yourself, as well as for those who hear the news.

Smart Move #242: Determine the Best Timing for Your Announcement

Not only do you need to find the best time to make your move, but you also need to determine the best time to let others know you're making a change. It's important not to jeopardize your current job or your professional relationships or reputation by announcing your intentions too early. It is generally advisable to keep quiet about your plans as long as possible. The rationale for doing so is that you want to be absolutely certain that you're going to go through with the career change and that you've made some progress toward your goals before you start announcing your news to others.

When you find, however, that keeping your transition a secret would hinder your progress toward making a change, then it is time to tell people. You might, for example, need to let your boss know what you're doing if you'll be unable to work late because you're taking a class. Whatever the situation, just make sure that it is absolutely necessary before you confide in your colleagues. You never know how they are going to react, even if you think you have good relationships with them.

Smart Move #243: Do Damage Control with Bosses and Colleagues

Professional colleagues will have varied reactions to the news that you are moving to a new career field. Some will be disappointed, some jealous, and some angry, while others will be genuinely happy for you. While you can't fully control people's reactions, you can try to avoid negative responses by being careful and thoughtful in the way you break the news to people. Don't gloat or speak negatively about the field or job you're leaving. And let them know that you have given very careful thought to your decision.

Smart Move #244: Break the News to Parents and Other Family Gently

Similar strategies to Smart Move #243 are advisable for telling parents, spouses, or other family members. The most common reaction that families have is one of concern that the decision is a rash one. It's therefore critical that you let your family know how much thought has gone into your decision. Be prepared to tell them how many people you've spoken to, how much research you've done, and how extensively you've evaluated your strengths and priorities. If you impress them with how thorough and responsible you've been in making your decision, most rational family members will support your decision.

PREPARATION

CHALLENGE: PREPARING FOR A SMOOTH AND SUCCESSFUL CAREER CHANGE

Madeleine decided to ignore all the advice she had gotten (that recommended she stay in her current job and slowly transition into her new business). She was so tired of going to her job at the accounting firm, and was so looking forward to starting her business, that she decided to resign with the usual two weeks notice. She had enough money saved up to live on for a few months, so she didn't anticipate any problems. Madeleine was confident that there was a big demand for the services she would offer and that her solid experience and academic credentials would attract clients. Well, unfortunately, Madeleine's plan didn't work out so well. It ended up taking her three full months and more money than she had expected just to get her business set up. She had not anticipated such hefty legal fees in establishing her company as the appropriate legal entity and had underestimated the cost of supplies and equipment. Madeleine didn't realize how long it would take to iron out the kinks in her daily business procedures. In addition, it took much longer to obtain the first client than she had expected. Before that first client came in, Madeleine had already used up all of her savings and could barely pay her rent.

Laying a Foundation for Your Transition

Even the brightest, most well-educated people can make some not-so-smart moves when it comes to changing careers. Whether you're starting your own business or just moving to a new career field, it is crucial that you take the time and make the effort to prepare for your transition. Just because you have good experience or an impressive education doesn't mean you will sail right into a new job, educational program, or successful business.

Smart Move #245: Review Your Transition Game Plan

Now is the time to go back to the transition game plan you established in the Timing section of this chapter. Take a look at the mini-steps you determined would be necessary for you to make your transition. Make sure that these still seem like the best way to go. Make any adjustments that seem necessary and then be prepared to stick with your plan. People often have a tendency to craft elaborate plans only to find that, when they actually start to take action, they ignore the plan. It's easy to get caught up in the excitement of the moment when you get your transition underway and forget to follow the plan you had laid out. So, keep your career change journal on hand and refer to it often to keep yourself on track.

Smart Move #246: Learn to Speak the Language of the New World

Entering a new career field or business is like entering a foreign country: It always helps to speak the local language. In career development terms, *language* can mean a couple of different things. First, it can be taken literally to mean the jargon or lexicon of people in the field you're moving into. Speaking like a native can put you in good stead when you interview for jobs, internships, or an educational program. *Language* can also be taken more figuratively to mean the overall culture, climate, or norms of your new field. Everything from how you dress to how you behave when networking can affect your likelihood of being accepted into that new world. If you're not sure how to get a handle on the language issue, refer to the smart moves offered in chapter 1.

Smart Move #247: Develop a Career Change Soundbyte

As mentioned in Smart Move #195, an important part of your vocabulary in this new language is a pitch, or a career change *soundbyte*—a brief statement that tells prospective employers (or clients if you plan to be self-employed) who you are, what you have to offer, and what you need from them.

Smart Move #248: Prepare Your Travel Papers

Just as you need a passport and perhaps a visa when travelling to other countries, you need specific documents when venturing from one career field to another. These can include resumes, bios, portfolios, letters of recommendation, and reference lists (or promotional materials if you're going into business for yourself). Putting these materials together, or updating old ones, is an extremely important step in preparing for a career change. It might take more time than you think, so be sure to start working on these early.

When making a career change, your old resume, for example, may no longer be relevant. You may need to change your job descriptions to emphasize your transferable skills and experience rather than focusing on the responsibilities that are specific to your old field.

TRANSITION RESOURCES

CHALLENGE: MAKING SURE YOU DON'T HAVE TO GO IT ALONE

After Madeleine's false start in her new business, she realized that she maybe didn't know everything she needed to know about running a business. Sure, she knew how to keep her business' books and file taxes, but she didn't know how to market her services, manage client relationships, or handle the day-to-day operations of her business. She was also embarrassed to find that she had miscalculated the expenses involved in starting and running her business even though she had a master's degree in accounting. Clearly, Madeleine needed to educate herself about setting up and running a small business if she was ever to achieve success.

INVOLVING PEOPLE AND INFORMATION IN YOUR TRANSITION

As Madeleine found, even smart, well-educated people can flounder when they venture into unfamiliar territory. A career change—whether into your own business or just a new career field—can be a daunting task. Like any challenging transition in life, it helps to go through a career change with the support of other people and the knowledge of what it takes to succeed in your new endeavor.

Smart Move #249: Rally a Support Team

Life's most challenging tasks are rarely solo efforts. The real movers and shakers of this world usually owe much of their success to an inner circle of supporters who keep them motivated and steer them in the right direction. Even if you're usually the most self-sufficient person in the world, making a career change is not the time to test the limits of your independence. Instead, it is a time to rally a support team around you.

A support team is important not only because multiple heads are better than one when it comes to brainstorming job searches or business development strategies, but also because everyone needs some degree of emotional support and encouragement when undergoing a life transition. Psychologists who study career development have found that the success of a transition is highly dependent on the strength of one's support system.

Your support team can include family, friends, and professional colleagues, as well as experts in career development. Career counselors, job search coaches, or small business advisors are just some of the experts who can help facilitate your transition. (They are discussed more in Smart Move #251.)

Smart Move #250: Revisit Your Alma Mater

Some of the best resources for a career transition can be found at the college or graduate school you attended (and occasionally, even at your high school). While the services offered in a campus career center vary from school to school, most have at least some of the following:

- Job Listings—Most career centers list full-time and part-time jobs either through a website that you can access from anywhere, in books, or on bulletin boards in the actual career office. Some career centers also publish newsletters for alumni that list jobs.

- Internships—While many internships listed in campus career centers may be offered only to current students, you should at least inquire about ones available to alumni. As with regular job listings, internships might be found on line, in the office, or in a newsletter.

- Alumni—Some career development offices have listings of alumni who have volunteered to serve as a resource for fellow alums. The names are often listed in books or computer databases you can look through on campus or are available by mail when you make a formal request for a search of alumni in a given geographical area and/ or career field. Occasionally, these listings are administered through the alumni relations office rather than the career center. Alumni can be an excellent addition to your networking efforts as you attempt to make a career change and might even be in a position to hire you or refer you to job openings (or to refer clients if you are self-employed).

- Career information library—As mentioned in chapter 7, guidebooks, magazines, professional journals, and trade papers are essential resources in a career change. Since your local public library may be lacking in career or job search resources, a college or graduate school career center can be a good place to find what you need. You may even be able to use the career office's library at a school you did not attend. So, if your alma mater(s) is far from where you live, call the career development offices of colleges and universities near you to see if any can offer you access to their libraries.

Smart Move #251: Enlist the Professionals

Whether they are regular members of your support team or simply people you consult with occasionally, career development professionals can be particularly valuable resources when you are making a career transition. You'll find that these professionals go by various titles—career counselors, career consultants, career strategists, career management consultants, executive coaches, or job search coaches. Some may focus more on the psychological aspects of a career change, helping you overcome internal roadblocks to decision-making or taking action. Others may focus on the strategy involved, helping you brainstorm ways to get from your old career to the new one. And still others might assist with only the nuts and bolts of your career change, perhaps helping you write your resume and cover letters, or prepare for interviews. A full-service career development professional will provide all of these services, or at least two out of the three. So, before setting an appointment with one, think about which areas of your career change you need the most help with and make sure that the person you'll be meeting with has expertise in those areas.

In addition to the professional organizations listed on pages 171 and 51, you can also check your local Yellow Pages phone directory under "Career Counseling" or "Vocational Counseling" to find an expert. Or even better, ask around among friends and professional colleagues to see if anyone can recommend a career counselor first-hand. Also, some college and universities offer career counseling services to alumni, either in-person or by phone.

Smart Move #252: Do More Research

Now that you're about to implement your career change (or are already in the midst of doing so), you might find that you don't have all the information you need to make the transition. You may wonder about whether it's really worthwhile to take classes, and if so, which ones. You might also have questions about the best way to get a job in the new field or how to redesign your resume. The research you did in books, online, and with people as suggested in chapter 7, may have given you enough information to identify and choose among your career change options. Now that you are actually acting on that choice, though, the results of your research might not provide all the answers you need. If that's the case, now is the time to go back to the people you spoke with or the other resources you used at the decision-making stage and find the information you need to implement this career change successfully.

Smart Move #253: Learn the Best Job-Search Techniques

If your career change involves looking for a new job (as opposed to applying to school or starting a business), then an important element of your transition resources will be advice on the most effective job-search techniques. This advice might come from the job search coaches and other career counselors mentioned in Smart Move #251 but can also be found in books and on line (you will also find ideas in other books and websites listed in the appendix). While it is always important that you go into a job search with a strategic plan and strategies, it is particularly essential to do so when you're making a career change. You need to make sure that the job search methods you use are appropriate for the new field. You also need to present yourself as the type of candidate that prospective employers in that field want to see, not as the type of person who gets hired in your old career field.

Tips and Twists for Job Searching When You're Making a Career Change

The following are some general rules-of-thumb for what works when you're making a career change. Keep in mind, though, that these are absolutely not hard–and–fast rules. Every job search is unique.

- You are more likely to get your job through networking than through answering ads or mailing out unsolicited resumes and cover letters.
- Your job search will probably take at least a few months longer (perhaps several months longer) than if you were looking for a job in your old career field.
- You may have to take a pay cut or stay at the same salary you've been earning rather than going up in pay. (But don't sell yourself short and assume you have to take a major cut!)
- You will most likely have to change your image—either dramatically or slightly—to fit into the culture of the new career field, so give some thought to how you should change your business attire, demeanor, etc.
- Your resume may need a summary or profile statement at the top of it that spells out for the reader what your transferable skills and experience are. This summary helps to de-emphasize your job titles and description (which come later on the resume) since these may not be as relevant to the new field. (See the books recommended in the Job Search section of the bibliography in the appendix for more guidance in writing this type of resume.)

ADJUSTING

CHALLENGE: ADJUSTING TO YOUR NEW CAREER

Craig was well underway with his career move into film when he started to have some second thoughts about his decision. He had been accepted into film school and had already completed two semesters. He was still working on the weekends for the documentary film company and now was being paid for his time rather than being a volunteer. To make extra money, Craig was also doing some private tutoring in writing and other areas related to his prior career as an English teacher and was working part time teaching English to recent immigrants in a nonprofit organization. His schedule was crazy, but somehow he managed to keep it all together and do well in his classes. Craig was getting impatient, though, and wondered if all the effort was worth it. He worried that he would never be successful in a competitive field like filmmaking. Craig also worried that he would never be able to get a steady job and pay off his debts. He even started having daydreams that maybe he should have become a stockbroker! Craig tried to remind himself that he had always wanted to be a documentary filmmaker and that he should be happy he was one year closer to reaching that goal, but he still found himself racked with anxiety and impatience.

BEING REALISTIC AND PATIENT

When you've finally made your move and find yourself in a new career, it's perfectly normal to have doubts about whether you've made the right decision or to be less than 100 percent satisfied in your new role. Adjusting to a new career takes time, patience, and effort—particularly when the new field is dramatically different from what you were in before or when there's a long period of dues-paying to get into it, as was the case with Craig. The smart moves that follow are some of the ways you can adjust to your new role.

Smart Move #254: Trust Your Decision-Making Abilities

If your concerns are primarily centered around whether you've made the right decision in the first place, try to review the steps that have led you to this point. If you carefully followed the suggestions offered in chapters 6 and 7, then you have probably made a good decision and have nothing to worry about. If you took a close look at why you wanted to get out of your old field, surveyed all the possible options for fields to transition into, and used effective decision-making techniques, then you certainly didn't make a rash move.

Also, remember that you did not make this decision completely on your own. Not only did you do research, but you also talked with people who helped you make your career change decision. So, if you're saying to yourself, "Am I crazy to have made this move?" remember that you had advice and input from others when you made your decision.

Smart Move #255: Don't Expect Miracles

Be sure your expectations are realistic. Did you expect this career change to transform your life? Make sure you're not expecting miracles. Remember that your work is only one part of your life. Sure, you may spend a lot of time on your job, but the things you do outside of work should bear some of the responsibility for your happiness. As you learned in Smart Move #217, "Disinguish Personal Problems from Professional Problems," it's important not to look to your work as the sole source of your happiness.

Also, keep in mind that rarely does any career choice feel perfect. It's a rare person who doesn't have some complaint about her career. So, if you were expecting 100 percent satisfaction, you were setting yourself up for disappointment. After all the thought and planning that undoubtedly went into your career choice, you may have built up an expectation that this new career would be perfect. But the "perfect career" may not even exist. So, be as realistic as possible in your expectations.

Smart Move #256: Learn from Past Mistakes

To make sure that you find satisfaction and success in your new career, try to learn from any past mistakes you may have made. If you've had difficulty in the past with any of the on-the-job or career management issues discussed in parts one and two of this book, keep those in the forefront of your mind. Don't assume they won't be problems now just because you've changed careers.

If you had trouble getting along with bosses or coworkers in the past, communicating clearly and appropriately, or with any other aspect of your career, then you may find that those problems pop up again. So, now that you're getting established in a new career, you may need to cycle back to the start of this book and review the smart moves recommended for dealing with your particular concerns.

Smart Move #257: Realize that Nothing is Permanent

If you really are unhappy in your new career and are certain you've made a big mistake, then don't despair. People have been known to make mistakes when choosing a new career, even if they were extremely careful in making the choice. Sometimes, no matter how carefully you think about what you want and how thoroughly you research the field you're moving into, you may find that once you get there, it's just not what you expected.

If this happens to you, realize that nothing is permanent. You might just need to make a slight shift within that field. Perhaps you're only in the wrong job, not the entirely wrong career field. Or, maybe you need to change the area of the field you're in, moving to a different industry or sector, for example. If you invested substantial time and money in this career change, then one of these minor shifts may be the answer rather than starting completely over in a whole new field.

If you really believe, though, that the whole career choice was a mistake, then another transition may be warranted. Remember, people change careers a lot these days, so there's nothing wrong with admitting that you made a mistake and moving on from there. Just be sure, though, that you've given this career every chance to work out. As you've learned in other smart moves, you need to be patient, keep your expectations realistic, and allow enough time to pass so that you can be sure you've given this career every possible chance to work for you.

Also, an important thing to keep in mind is that your dissatisfaction may reflect the fact that initial jobs in a new career field are often not as interesting, exciting, and challenging as future positions you'll move into. You might have gotten used to having responsibility and challenge in your old career and now find yourself in a position that's a bit below your ability level, but it's the job you had to take to get your foot in the door of the new field. If that's the case, you just need to look at this initial stage as a time to pay your dues and use the smart moves recommended in chapters 3, 4, and 5 to work on getting ahead as fast as you can.

Smart Move #258: Congratulate Yourself

Whether you're having doubts everyday or are deliriously happy in your new career, don't forget to acknowledge the major transition you've made. Making a career change takes perseverance, courage, and a lot of effort. Many people complain about their jobs or careers but never do anything about it. Or, they decide to make a change, get halfway through it, then let their efforts fizzle out. If you not only whine and moan about your career but also have the nerve and initiative to do something about it, then you deserve congratulations. So, give yourself a pat on the back for getting this far, and enjoy your new job.

Recommended Books for Working Smart

CAREER MANAGEMENT (GENERAL)

Maslach, Christina and Michael P. Leiter. *The Truth About Burnout*. San Francisco, California: Jossey-Bass Publishers, 1997.

McKena, Elizabeth Perle. *When Work Doesn't Work Anymore: Women, Work and Identity*. New York: Delacorte Press, 1997.

Reinhold, Barbara Bailey. *Toxic Work: How to Overcome Stress, Overload, and Burnout and Revitalize Your Career*. New York: Plume, 1997.

Stevenson, Ollie and Dana Huebler. *The Colorblind Career: What Every AfricanAmerican, Hispanic–American, and Asian–American Needs to Succeed in Today's Tough Job Market*. Princeton, NJ: Peterson's, 1997.

IMAGE

Bird, Polly. *Sell Yourself: Persuasive Tactics to Boost Your Image (Institute of Management Series)*. London: Pitman Publishing Ltd., 1994.

Bixler, Susan and Nancy Nix-Rice. *The New Professional Image: From Corporate Casual to the Ultimate Power Look*. Holbrook, MA: Adams Media, 1997.

Bramson, Robert M. *What Your Boss Doesn't Tell You Until It's Too Late: How to Correct Behavior That Is Holding You Back.* New York: Fireside, 1996.

Gross, Kim Johnson. *Work Clothes: Casual Dress for Serious Work.* New York: Knopf, 1996.

Toogood, Granville N. *The Articulate Executive: Learn to Look, Act, and Sound Like a Leader.* New York: McGraw-Hill, 1997.

COMMUNICATION

Axtell, Roger and Mike Fornwald. *Do's and Taboos of Public Speaking: How to Get Those Butterflies Flying in Formations.* New York: John Wiley & Sons, 1992.

Benjamin, Susan. *Words at Work: Business Writing in Half the Time With Twice the Power.* Reading, MA: Addison-Wesley Publishing Co., 1997.

Booher, Dianna. *Communicate With Confidence!: How to Say It Right the First Time and Every Time.* New York: McGraw Hill, 1994.

Bozek, Phillip. *50 One-Minute Tips to Better Communication: A Wealth of Business Communication Ideas.* Menlo Park, CA: Crisp Publications, 1997.

Dee, David and Diana Bryan (Illustrator). *Telephone Terrific!: Facts, Fun, and 103 "How-To" Tips for Phone Success.* Chicago: Dartnell Corp., 1994.

Friedman, Nancy J. *Telephone Skills from A to Z.* Menlo Park, CA: Crisp Publications, 1995.

Griffin, Jack. *The Complete Handbook of Model Business Letters.* Engelwood Cliffs, NJ: Prentice Hall Trade, 1997.

Heller, Bernard. *The 100 Most Difficult Business Letters You'll Ever Have to Write, Fax, or E-Mail.* New York: HarperCollins, 1994.

Mira, Thomas K. *Negotiate Smart.* New York: Princeton Review/ Random House, 1995.

Robinson, Adam. *Word Smart.* New York: Princeton Review/Random House, 1996.

Ruskin, Mark. *Speaking Up: What to Say to Your Boss and Everyone Else Who Gets on Your Case.* Holbrook, MA: Adams, 1993.

Tannen, Deborah. *That's Not What I Meant!: How Conversational Style Makes or Breaks Your Relations With Others.* New York: Ballantine, 1991.

Weiss, Donald H. *Why Didn't I Say That?!: What to Say and How to Say it in Tough Situations on the Job.* New York: AMACOM, 1996.

Weiss, Lynn and Lora Cain. *Power Lines: What to Say in 250 Problem Situations.* NewYork: Harper, 1995.

Westheimer, Patricia. *The Perfect Memo! Write Your Way to Career Success.* Indianapolis, IN: JIST Works, Inc., 1997.

Protocol/Business Etiquette

Axtell, Roger. *Do's and Taboos Around the World.* New York: John Wiley & Sons, 1993.

Axtell, Roger. *Do's and Taboos Around the World for Women in Business.* New York: John Wiley & Sons, 1997.

Baldrige, Letitia. *Letitia Baldrige's New Complete Guide to Executive Manners.* New York: Scribner, 1993.

Craig, Elizabeth and Betty Craig. *Don't Slurp Your Soup: A Basic Guide to Business Etiquette.* St. Paul, MN: Brighton Publications, 1996.

Maloff, Chalda and Susan MacDuff Wood. *Business and Social Etiquette with Disabled People: A Guide to Getting Along with Persons Who Have Impairments of Mobility, Vision, Hearing or Speech.* Springfield, IL: Charles C. Thomas Pub. Ltd., 1988.

Yamada, Haru. *Different Games, Different Rules: Why Americans and Japanese Misunderstand Each Other.* New York: Oxford University Press, 1997.

Teamwork/Meetings

Miller, Robert F. and Marilyn Pincus. *Running A Meeting That Works* (Barron's Business Success Series). Hauppage, NY: Barrons Educational Series, 1997.

Mosvick, Robert K. and Robert B. Nelson. *We've Got to Start Meeting Like This: A Guide to Successful Meeting Management.* Indianapolis, IN: JIST Works, Inc., 1996.

Rees, Fran. *Teamwork from Start to Finish.* San Francisco, CA: Jossey-Bass, 1997.

Sonneman, Milly. *Beyond Words: A Guide to Drawing Out Ideas for Anyone Who Works With Groups.* Berkeley, CA: Ten Speed Press, 1997.

Organizational Culture and Politics

Adams, Scott. *The Dilbert Principle: A Cubicle's-Eye View of Bosses, Meetings, Management Fads & Other Workplace Afflictions.* New York: HarperCollins, 1996.

Bridges, W. *Job Shift.* Reading, MA: Addison-Wesley Publishing, 1994.

Clark, Ann D. and Patt Perkins. *Surviving Your Boss: How to Cope With Office Politics and Get on With Your Job.* Secaucus, NJ: Citadel Press, 1996.

Douglas, Mary. *How Institutions Think.* Syracuse, NY: Syracuse University Press, 1986.

Felder, Leonard. *Does Someone At Work Treat You Badly?/ How to Handle Brutal Bosses, Crazy Coworkers...and Anyone Else Who Drives You Nuts.* New York: Berkley Publishing Group, 1993.

Kirschner, Rick and Rick Brinkman. *Dealing with People You Can't Stand: How to Bring Out the Best in People at Their Worst.* New York: McGraw-Hill, 1994.

Kotter, John P. and James L. Heskett. *Corporate Culture and Performance.* New York: Free Press, 1992.

Krebbs-Hirsh, Sandra and Jane A.C. Kise. *Work It Out: Clues for Solving People Problems at Work.* Palo Alto, CA: Consulting Psychologists Press, 1996.

Lareau, William. *Dancing With the Dinosaur: Learning to Live in the Corporate Jungle.* Winchester, New Hampshire: Winchester Press, 1997.

Wilson-Schaef, Anne and Diane Fassel. *The Addictive Organization: Why We Overwork, Cover Up, Pick Up the Pieces, Please the Boss and Perpetuate Sick Organizations.* San Francisco, CA: Harper San Francisco, 1990.

Yate, Martin. *Beat the Odds.* New York: Ballantine Books, 1995.

NETWORKING

Encyclopedia of Associations. Gale Research Company, (annual).

Heenehan, Margaret. *Networking (Job Notes Series).* New York: Princeton Review/Random House, 1997.

NTPA: National Trade and Professional Associations of the United States. Columbia Books, (annual).

Tullier, Michelle. *Networking for Everyone: Connecting with People for Career and Job Success.* Indianapolis, IN: JIST Works, 1998.

UNEMPLOYMENT

Albright, Townsend. *How to Hold It All Together: When You've Lost Your Job.* Lincolnwood, IL: VGM Career Horizons, 1996.

Dubrin, Andrew J. *Bouncing Back: How to Stay in the Game When Your Career is on the Line.* New York: McGraw-Hill, 1991.

Elkort, Martin. *Getting from Fired to Hired: Bounce Back from Losing Your Job and Get Your Career Back on Track.* New York: Prentice Hall/Arco Publishing, 1997.

Pulley, Mary Lynn. *Losing Your Job, Reclaiming Your Soul.* San Francisco, CA: Jossey-Bass, 1997.

SELF-EMPLOYMENT

Abarbanel, Karin. *How to Succeed on Your Own.* New York: Henry Holt & Co., 1994.

Faux, Marian. *Successful Freelancing: The Complete Guide to Establishing and Running Any Kind of Freelance Business.* New York: St. Martin's Press, 1997.

Gilkerson, Linda and Theresia Paauwe. *Self-Employment: From Dream to Reality: Planning for Microenterprises.* Indianapolis, IN: JIST Works, 1997.

Hakim, Cliff. *We Are All Self-Employed.* San Francisco, CA: Berrett-Koehler, 1995.

Holtz, Herman. *The Complete Guide to Being an Independent Contractor.* Chicago, IL: Upstart Publishing, 1995.

Lonier, Terri. *Working Solo.* New Paltz, NY: Portico Press, 1994.

Lonier, Terri. *Working Solo Sourcebook.* New Paltz, NY: Portico Press, 1995.

CHOOSING CAREERS

Boldt, Laurence. *Zen and the Art of Making a Living.* New York: Penguin USA, 1993.

Edwards, P. and S. Edwards. *Finding Your Perfect Work.* New York: G.P. Putnam & Sons, 1996.

Mantis, Hillary. *Alternative Careers for Lawyers.* New York: Princeton Review / Random House, 1997.

Sher, Barbara. *I Could Do Anything if Only I Knew What it Was.* New York: Bantam Doubleday Dell, 1995.

Sher, Barbara. *Wishcraft: How to Get What You Really Want.* New York: Ballantine Books, 1986.

Tieger, Paul and Barbara Barron-Tieger. *Do What You Are.* New York: Little, Brown & Co., 1995.

Yate, Martin. *Career Smarts: Jobs with a Future.* New York: Ballantine Books, 1997.

RESEARCHING CAREERS

Encyclopedia of Associations. Gale Research Company, (annual).

Farr, J. Michael. *America's Top Jobs for College Graduates,* 2nd Edition. Indianapolis, IN: JIST Works, 1997.

Farr, J. Michael. *America's Top Medical, Education, & Human Services Jobs,* 3rd Edition. Indianapolis, IN: JIST Works, 1997.

Farr, J. Michael. *America's Top Office, Management, Sales, & Professional Jobs,* 3rd Edition. Indianapolis, IN: JIST Works, 1997.

Krannich, Ronald and Caryl Krannich. *Best Jobs for the 1990s and into the 21st Century.* Manassas Park, VA: Impact, 1993.

NTPA: National Trade and Professional Associations of the United States. Columbia Books (annual).

U.S. Department of Labor, *Dictionary of Occupational Titles*, (annual).

U.S. Department of Labor, *Occupational Outlook Handbook*, (annual).

Yate, Martin. *Career Smarts: Jobs with a Future*. New York: Ballantine Books, 1997.

Job Search

Haft, Tim. *Resumes (Job Notes Series)*. New York: Princeton Review/Random House, 1997.

Haft, Tim. *Trashproof Resumes*. New York: Princeton Review/Random House, 1995.

Jandt, Fred E. and Mary B. Nemnich. *Using the Internet and the World Wide Web in Your Job Search*. Indianapolis, IN: JIST Work, 1997.

Kimeldorf, Martin. *Portfolio Power*. Princeton, NJ: Peterson's, 1997.

Taub, Marci. *Interviews (Job Notes Series)*. New York : Princeton Review/Random House, 1997.

Tullier, Michelle. *Cover Letters (Job Notes Series)*. New York: Princeton Review/Random House, 1997.

Tullier, Michelle; Haft, Tim; Heenehan, Margaret; and Taub, Marci. *Job Smart*. New York: Princeton Review/Random House, 1997.

Wendleton, Kate. *Targeting the Job You Want*. New York: Five O'Clock Books, 1997.

Wendleton, Kate. *Through the Brick Wall: How to Job Hunt in a Tight Market*. New York: Villard Press, 1992.

Witt, Melanie Astaire. *Job Strategies for People with Disabilities*. Princeton, NJ: Peterson's, 1992.

Change/Transitions

Bardwick, J.M. *The Plateauing Trap*. New York: AMACOM, 1986.

Brehony, K.A. *Awakening at Midlife*. New York: Riverhead Books, 1996.

Hall, Douglas T. and Associates. *The Career is Dead: Long Live the Career*. San Francisco, CA: Jossey-Bass, 1996.

Howard, Ann. *The Changing Nature of Work*. San Francisco, CA: Jossey-Bass, 1995.

Knaus, William J. *Change Your Life Now: Powerful Techniques for Positive Change*. New York: John Wiley & Sons, 1994.

Simon, Sidney B. *Getting Unstuck: Breaking Through Your Barriers to Change*. New York: Warner Books, 1988.

Recommended Web Sites for Working Smart

About Work

www.aboutwork.com

America's Employer's: The Job Seeker's "Home"

www.americasemployers.com

America's Job Bank

www.ajb.dni.us:80/

Career Action Center

www.careeraction.org

Career Center for Workforce Diversity

www.eop.com

Career Magazine

www.careermag.com

Career Mosaic

www.careermosaic.com

Career Toolbox

www.careertoolbox.com

CAREERXROADS

www.careerxroads.com

EOP

www.eop.com

Help Wanted-USA

iccweb.com/employ.html

Hoovers Online

www.hoovers.com

JobWeb

www.jobweb.org

100 Best Companies for Working Mothers

www.women.com

The Monster Board

www.monster.com

The Reilly Guide

www.jobtrak.com/jobguide/

Women's Professional Directory

www.womensdirectory.com

Index

ABOUT THE AUTHORS

Marci I. Taub is a career counselor in private practice based in New Jersey. She specializes in on-site and long-distance career counseling and testing, job search coaching, and educational advising services for clients from teens through early thirties. She is the co-author of *Job Smart* and the author of *Job Notes: Interviews* (both published by The Princeton Review/Random House, 1997). She has been an adjunct faculty member of New York University's School of Continuing Education, teaching courses through the Center for Career, Education, and Life Planing. Her professional affiliations include memberships in the american Counseling Association and the National Career Development Association. Marci holds an M.A. in Counseling from Montclair State University, a Certificate in Adult Career Planning and Development from New York University, and a B.A. from Oberlin College. Prior to entering private practice, Marci consulted and was employed in human resources with major financial institutions. She also held positions on colleges in New York and New Jersey, advising students on career planning and job search issues. Marci can be reached at marcitaub@aol.com.

Michelle Tullier has been a career counselor in universities and private practice since 1985, advising adults of all ages on career choice and job search issues. Through her New York City-based practice, which attracts clients from across the country and abroad, she specializes in the career development needs of high school and college students, recent graduates, and young professionals in their twenties and thirties. Michelle holds a Ph.D. in counseling psychology from UCLA and a B.A. from Wellesley College. She is on the faculty of New York University's School of Continuing Education where she teaches beginning and experienced career consultants, and was a career counselor at Barnard College of Columbia University for several years. Michelle is the co-author of *Job Smart* and the author of *Job Notes: Cover Letters* (both published by The Princeton Review/Random House, 1997) and *Networking for Everyone* (JIST Works, 1998). Michelle serves as a Career Committee Chair for the Independent Educational Consultants Association (IECA) and is a frequent public speaker, seminar leader, and consultant. She can be reached at CareerDr@aol.com.

NOTES

NOTES

NOTES

NOTES

NOTES

NOTES

NOTES

NOTES

NOTES

NOTES

FIND US...

International

Hong Kong
4/F Sun Hung Kai Centre
30 Harbour Road, Wan Chai,
Hong Kong
Tel: (011)85-2-517-3016

Japan
Fuji Building 40, 15-14
Sakuragaokacho, Shibuya Ku,
Tokyo 150, Japan
Tel: (011)81-3-3463-1343

Korea
Tae Young Bldg, 944-24,
Daechi- Dong, Kangnam-Ku
The Princeton Review- ANC
Seoul, Korea 135-280,
South Korea
Tel: (011)82-2-554-7763

Mexico City
PR Mex S De RL De Cv
Guanajuato 228 Col. Roma
06700 Mexico D.F., Mexico
Tel: 525-564-9468

Montreal
666 Sherbrooke St.
West, Suite 202
Montreal, QC H3A 1E7 Canada
Tel: (514) 499-0870

Pakistan
1 Bawa Park - 90 Upper Mall
Lahore, Pakistan
Tel: (011)92-42-571-2315

Spain
Pza. Castilla, 3 - 5° A, 28046
Madrid, Spain
Tel: (011)341-323-4212

Taiwan
155 Chung Hsiao East Road
Section 4 - 4th Floor,
Taipei R.O.C., Taiwan
Tel: (011)886-2-751-1243

Thailand
Building One, 99 Wireless Road
Bangkok, Thailand 10330
Tel: (662) 256-7080

Toronto
1240 Bay Street, Suite 300
Toronto M5R 2A7 Canada
Tel: (800) 495-7737
Tel: (716) 839-4391

Vancouver
4212 University Way NE,
Suite 204
Seattle, WA 98105
Tel: (206) 548-1100

National (U.S.)
We have over 60 offices around the U.S. and
run courses in over 400 sites. For courses and locations
within the U.S. call 1 (800) 2/Review and you will be
routed to the nearest office.

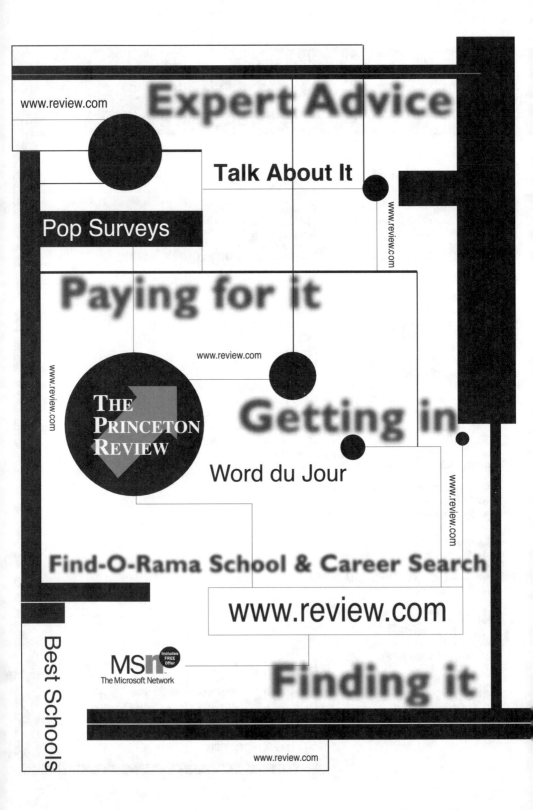

WHAT AM I GOING TO DO?

We can help you answer that question, whether you're just getting out of college, have a graduate degree, or simply want to change your career path.